YANKEE'S GUIDE TO FLORIDA GARDENING

by

Hank and Marlene Bruce

Dedicated to our daughter, Karen,
the brightest flower in our garden.

ISBN 0-932855-45-8

Published by Winner Enterprises
Post Office Box 151085
Altamonte Springs, FL 32715
Phone (407) 695-9000
Fax (407) 695-9014

Illustrations and Cover Photos by Hank & Marlene Bruce
Editorial: Erv Lampert
Design and Typesetting: Techware Corporation
Created on an Apple® Macintosh computer

Printed in the United States of America

NOTES FROM THE AUTHORS

Why a book on Florida gardening for Yankee's?

The answer is simple. When we moved here we found that every book, manual or guide we found assumed that we were natives or at least long term residents who already understood the climate, were familiar with semi-tropical plants and had a thorough knowledge of all the critters we ran into when we stepped out the back door.

We soon found that we were not alone in this sense of bewilderment; many other transplants were as confused and baffled as we were. Our goal is to provide a little insight into this strange world where orange trees and alligators can be found in the backyard and we pick tomatoes in January.

We tried to keep the information light and readable, hopefully even enjoyable. There are even a few quizzes included to make a rainy day more entertaining.

You are encouraged to read this book with these three suggestions in mind:

1. Don't take gardening too seriously. It should be fun, a source of relaxation and a way to relieve stress.

2. You will be far more successful with your own personal great outdoors if you cooperate rather than compete with Mamma Nature.

3. Gardening shouldn't be a religion. Avoid getting yourself all tied up with doctrine and absolute rules. Experiment on your own. There is always more than one right way to do almost anything. If it works for you what difference does it make what the experts say? If you don't agree with something we say in this book that's okay too. It's your backyard, not ours.

We don't offer this book to you as the final authority. In fact, we hope this is only the beginning for you. There are thousands of plants you can grow in Florida, and many more are introduced each year. We can only mention a few of them here. You can find a multitude of new and different varieties if you visit some of the truly magnificent botanical gardens and arboreta to be found in this state. The agricultural extension office nearest you is only a phone call away, all good garden centers and nurseries have experts that can offer advice and the local library is a treasure-trove of information. These are all valuable sources just waiting to make you a FLORIDA SMART GARDENER.

A book isn't written in a vacuum; it takes a lot of help and encouragement. We would like to thank the multitude of growers and retailers who have worked diligently to bring the finest in quality and variety to the public. They provided us with quality advice and counsel. A thanks is also in order to the researchers and instructors in the Florida university system for the never-ending research that constantly produces better plants, methods and techniques. These are the folks that have the answers to your questions when you call on the local extension office, and they also had the answers for us when we needed help. Lastly we would like to thank Erv Lampert, our editor and publisher, for his encouragement and patience while we labored on this project. A special thanks also to the Yankee's and other newcomers who, hopefully, will read this book and enjoy the experience of Florida gardening.

Most Florida gardening guides make reference to two ways of dividing the state into regions or zones. While plants recommended for, as an example, central Florida might do well a little north of the vague line between north and central or sub-tropical shrubs might be doing well in St. Petersburg, these maps and divisions are a good general guide. Remember, there will always be exceptions. These might be due to micro-climate, new improved or hardier varieties, even the extra effort you put into cold or heat protection can extend these ranges.

1. FLORIDA REGION MAP

   N - North Florida
   C - Central Florida
   S - South Florida
   ST -Semi (or Sub) Tropical

2. The United States Department of Agriculture has established a HARDINESS ZONE MAP based on the range of average annual minimum temperatures. This is what the Zone 7-9 refers to in your seed and nursery catalogs. Florida, being a large state, has four zones.

Zone 8—10° to 20° is the range of average minimum temperatures.
Zone 9—20° to 30° is the range of average minimum temperatures.
Zone 10—30° to 40° is the range of average minimum temperatures.
Zone 11—40° to 50° is the range of average minimum temperatures.

FLORIDA REGIONS

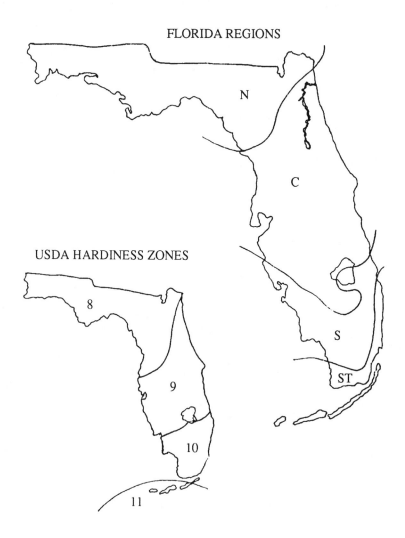

N

C

S

ST

USDA HARDINESS ZONES

8

9

10

11

YANKEE'S GUIDE TO FLORIDA GARDENING

TABLE OF CONTENTS

Coconut Palm
(Cocos nucifera)

FIRST IMPRESSIONS AND SECOND THOUGHTS

If you were like most Yankees, when you first moved to this state you were firmly convinced that Florida is a lush tropical paradise. You had visions of Fantasy Island, right? This expectation is understandable because you had been here on vacation and spent idyllic weeks at a fabulously landscaped resort. Your first impressions of Florida went something like this:

1.   Florida is a land of swaying palms, usually surrounding a motel.

2.   Trees never lose their leaves in this southern Camelot; after all there is no winter.

3.   The fragrance of orange blossoms and jasmine always hangs heavy in the air.

4.   The climate is so conducive to plant growth that a walking stick left outside overnight will take root by morning and be in bloom within a week.

However, beauty and bounty don't just happen in Florida either. This is a state of abundance for the gardener, but it is an abundance of both opportunities and challenges. After the first impressions come the second thoughts. These are caused by a series of revelations:

1.   The Florida bugs are bigger, hungrier and more plentiful than anywhere up north.

2.   The grass is shy and retiring down here. Beautiful Florida lawns grow on sweat.

3.   There is no soil in Florida, only sand. If you want soil you have to make it yourself.

4.	Nematodes are a reality, even though you can't see them. The bright side is that they give you an easy excuse when something doesn't grow.

5.	Floridians don't dig glads, caladiums and dahlias for winter storage, but they do dig tulips, hyacinths and daffodils and keep them in the refrigerator all summer.

The truth of Florida gardening lies somewhere between these first impressions and second thoughts. There is an unparalleled diversity of plant material here for you to draw from because this is a transitional climate where both temperate and tropical plants can thrive. Florida's mild climate doesn't chase the gardener indoors for months at a time with snow and wind. Here the flowers really do bloom twelve months a year, if you plant the right flowers.

There are so many differences between here and the North that it does take time to become accustomed to them. After you have been in Florida for awhile you begin to miss some of the old friends from back home. We don't mean neighbors and relatives, we are referring to lilacs and fragrant flowering crabapple trees. You will think longingly of forsythias and pussy willows, rhododendrons and blue spruce. You encounter strange unfamiliar plants here every day and the stuff you used to nurse along on the windowsill up there grows with reckless abandon in your neighbor's backyard down here.

This book is designed to help you turn this homesickness into some nice memories and eliminate some of the confusion. We want to introduce you to year-round flowers, orange trees in the backyard, exotic fragrances and the Florida equivalents of some of the old familiar plants you left behind.

YANKEE CONVERSION CHART

When we move to Florida we leave behind some good friends and it's difficult to imagine living without blue spruce, bleeding hearts and some of your favorites. For that reason we have started the Yankee Conversion Chart. We would welcome your suggestions and additions to this effort to make Florida gardening more like home.

UP NORTH WE HAD	IN FLORIDA WE SUBSTITUTE
Clematis	Passion vine
Lilac	Crape myrtle
Forsythia	Thryalis
Bleeding heart	Clerodendrum vine
Lily of the valley	Liriope, turf lily
Tulips	Amaryllis
Colorado blue spruce	Norfolk Island pine
Bearded iris	African iris

The African iris (Moraea (Dietes) iridoides) isn't quite the bearded iris we grew up north, but at least it blooms almost all year and has few pest problems.

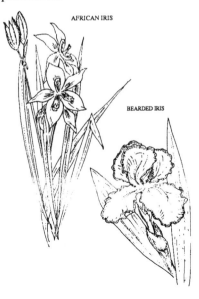

AFRICAN IRIS

BEARDED IRIS

SECTION ONE

THE BLOOMIN' LANDSCAPE

BEDDING PLANTS ARE FOR ALL SEASONS IN FLORIDA

Do you remember May up north? All the garden centers were overflowing with flats of marigolds, petunias and dozens of other bright colorful annuals. The great splashes of red, pink and yellow in the discount store parking lots meant spring had arrived. Then June came and the few remaining bedding plants were cleared out and you knew it was summer, and the time for planting was over.

There is a simple cycle in the north. You plant in the spring, enjoy those plants in the summer (by weeding, feeding, spraying and trimming), clean out the beds in the fall after the first killing frost, then look forward to the first snowfall of winter and building snowmen with the kids.

FLORIDA SEASONS

Now that you have relocated to paradise, the Yankee seasonal cycle no longer applies. Florida provides an almost unbelievable opportunity to be creative with your flowering beds and borders because they can be changed with the seasons. Some experts claim Florida has two seasons: a cool one running from October to April and a warm season that lasts from April to October. Other authorities argue that there are four distinct seasons: fall (October-December), winter (December-February), spring (February-May) and summer (May-September). Regardless of which expert you choose to agree with, there are several important factors a Yankee needs to keep in mind as he or she plans and plants the Florida flower beds and borders.

1.   In the north the gardening year begins in the spring. In Florida the planting year really begins in the autumn. Winter is the heavy stress month for plants in the north, but summer is the survival test here.

Autumn is a time of recovery from summer stress instead of death and destruction from a heavy frost. Autumn in Florida brings cooler temperatures that are easier on both the gardener and the garden. Spring is the time of renewal in the northern states, but here both spring and fall are seasons of rebirth.

2.   We don't have an almost violent explosion of spring in Florida. Remember how in the north spring happens all in a rush as a few warm days erase the snow? As if by magic yellow coltsfoot and little pink spring beauties dot the roadside while only days later plum trees, redbud and dogwood are showing their colors.

Florida has spring, but it seems less spectacular because here there is a floral happening fifty-two weeks a year. We are confronted with an ever-changing panorama of color and fragrance as each annual, perennial, shrub, tree and vine comes into it's full glory.

Autumn is not the dramatic Technicolor extravaganza in Florida that you were accustomed to in New England either because it is not the end of a growing season as much as it is a transition from one growing season to another.

3.   In the north you planted almost all of your annuals in the spring for summer bloom, but in Florida you will have the opportunity to grow petunias, pansies and snapdragons as well as many others during the cooler winter months, but these don't survive the stress of summer's heat and humidity well. For the weather that drives you to the air conditioning and iced tea we have the heat tolerant plants like purslane, vinca and begonias that bloom and thrive in the summer sun.

4.   We would like to clarify something of a misconception that many of us carry over from our northern gardens. We think it is the frost that puts an end to the flower beds, and since we may go an entire year without frost in many parts of Florida, the newly transplanted Yankee expects the flower beds to go on forever. For the most part it isn't a frost that destroys happily blooming annuals; it is the natural completion of their life cycle.

Annuals, by definition, are plants that germinate from seed, grow to maturity, flower and produce seed for the next generation all in one growing season. The alyssum, cosmos, marigolds and a host of others complete their mission in life, and as is the natural order of things, give up that life and become mulch. They return to the soil for the benefit of the next generation. Their nutrients and fibers are the inheritance they leave for their kids, the seeds of next season.

It doesn't matter whether that annual grew in the summer of Michigan or the winter of Florida; when it's life cycle is complete it is done. This is one of the reasons why we can replant the flower beds several times a year in Florida. That life cycle may run four, five or six months, but when it is over we replant for the next season.

5.   Not all of your favorite bedding plants are annuals. You remember with a certain fondness some of those favorites of the northern clime like peonies, primrose, Virginia bluebells and bearded iris. These plants would die down each autumn (sometimes sooner than that), and reappear next spring for their moment in the sun. By definition a perennial will live, grow and flower for several years. Some of the plants that we grew as annuals in the north are perennials in their native habitat. These plants (like begonias, some gaillardias, purslane and vinca) may continue to thrive and bloom from season to season if they do not encounter harsh weather or cold temperatures. Many of these are what met their doom in a killing frost.

HOW THE PROFESSIONAL LANDSCAPERS USE THE COLOR OF BEDDING PLANTS IN FLORIDA

Almost everything you did with blooming annuals in the North you can do in Florida. The following are some suggestions from the pros you might find helpful:

1.   Flower beds and borders are most effective when you don't mix too many colors or varieties. It is this massed planting that makes the resorts' landscaping so striking.

2.   Grass will not grow well in shade, but there is a wealth of flowering and foliage material that will. Light to moderate shade is tolerated by begonias, coleus, impatiens, vinca, dusty miller, pansies and ageratum to name a few.

3.   The pros also advise that when you plant your flower beds use low growing material or foliage as an edging to accent the featured color.

4.   Many homeowners new to this state aren't fully aware of the seasonal cycle and seem to be reluctant to change the plant material in their flowering beds and borders. When you leave the old plants in place beyond their prime you miss the opportunity to change color scheme, get the best plants for the season and also avoid the potential spread of insects and disease that comes from plants being in one place too long. It's like moving the furniture around in the living room. It can give the entire landscape a new look.

5.   Plan and plant where irrigation is convenient, drainage isn't a problem and the plantings will not interfere with traffic flow.

6.   Don't overlook planters, window boxes, decorative pots, urns and raised beds as sites for seasonal color. These decorative containers will enhance the charm and beauty of your home when filled to overflowing with ever blooming annuals, foliage or vines. One word of caution is in order here. Make certain that these pots and planters have drainage holes so excess water can escape. Root rot kills quickly.

7.   Annuals in hanging baskets can be a year-long color spectacular in Florida, but plants in containers tend to dry out quickly in this subtropical heat. You will need to water almost daily and feed with a water-soluble, bloom-builder type fertilizer every couple weeks. Don't be afraid to trim these container plants back severely to avoid a gangly adolescent appearance and encourage flowering.

8.   Cut flowers look great in the house and in Florida your flower beds can give you a perpetual supply. It's good for the plants to be pruned back occasionally and you get free flowers for your lady friends and neighbors.

9. Fragrance is a bonus with such plants as alyssum, petunias, nicotiana, carnations and dianthus to name only a few. The pros recommend planting these by the window or screen room where they can be enjoyed while you relax.

10. Plan before you plant. Study the charts in this book, then talk to knowledgeable nursery staff. Plan for color, season, insect and disease threat, necessary sunlight, moisture requirements, and most importantly, what YOU WANT.

PREPARING YOUR FLORIDA FLOWER BED

In Florida good rich topsoil doesn't just happen. Most likely the site of your future floral wonderland is a patch of sandy soil totally without socially redeeming qualities. It probably doesn't have much in the way of nutrients and organic matter either. The ideal soil is rich in good stuff. We're talking about decomposed plant parts (like rotted leaves, decayed roots left in the soil by previous inhabitants) compost and animal manures.

Organic matter in the soil serves several important functions.

1. There is some nutrient value so it is a food source.

2. It helps to hold moisture in the soil.

3. By holding this moisture it also helps to retain dissolved nutrients from applied fertilizers. This makes your fertilizer program more efficient.

4. By holding moisture and nutrients in the soil, organic matter encourages strong healthy root development.

5. Large amounts of organic material in the soil seem to help keep the nematode population in check by encouraging the growth of natural predators.

ORGANIC SOIL CONDITIONERS TO CHOOSE FROM

Hopefully this has convinced you that the addition of organic soil conditioners is necessary. Now you have to decide which one to use. Here are some of your options.

1.   Sphagnum (Canadian) peat — This is the brown stuff that can be found in heavy bales of various sizes. This is our favorite because it will absorb several times it's own weight in water, is usually not acid, contains few weed seeds and few disease problems are transmitted in this material. It may look expensive but it is sold by volume not weight so it goes farther than a bag of seemingly cheaper material that is sold by weight and may be over 50% water.

2.   Organic peat — This is the black or muck peat that you found up north in bags labeled Michigan Peat. It is usually sold in 40 or 50 pound bags. The pH can vary dramatically, will contain a wide variety of weed seeds and may harbor fungus diseases. When added to the soil it breaks down quicker than sphagnum peat does.

3.   Animal manures are an excellent soil conditioner and they contain some nutrients as a bonus. Don't rely on packaged manures as the only nutrient source for your plants because the food value is diminished when the manufacturer uses organic peat as an extender. Read the label before you buy.

4.   Sawdust is a good conditioner if it is decomposed, otherwise it will pull nitrogen from the soil as it breaks down.

5.   Sewage sludge, leaf mold and mushroom manure are just a few of the other alternatives that are easy to obtain and inexpensive.

6.   Compost — An excellent source of organic matter that you can make yourself. Weeds, grass clippings, the deceased from garden and landscape can all find their way into your compost pile.

Now you are ready to make soil. Before you start you may want to do a soil test to determine acidity. If the pH is below 6.0 you may want to add some dolomitic lime. See Section Four for details on soil acidity and correction.

You have your basic sandy Florida soil and your chosen organic conditioner; now all you have to do is mix them together. We recommend a blend of 50% Florida soil and 50% sphagnum peat or compost, but this is only one of many good options.

Many texts tell you to work the soil in a flower bed to a depth of about six inches. You can encourage much stronger root systems and increase drought tolerance if you go at least eight to twelve inches deep.

As you are mixing the conditioner and the soil you can add a good 100% organic fertilizer like 6-6-6 or 12-4-8 at the rate of approximately two cups per 100 square feet. This little snack will help get your new plants off to a good start.

PERENNIALS IN THE FLORIDA LANDSCAPE

Perennials are nothing new to the Yankee gardener, but now that you have moved to this fair state you will miss old friends like the magnificent bearded iris, the massive peonies and the petite lilies-of-the-valley; all those magnificent plants that made spring such a dramatic event.

To refresh your memory, perennials are plants that grow and flourish for several years or more. When we use the term 'perennial', we are usually referring to the plants that may go dormant with the coming of shorter days or winter weather. Then, with spring as inspiration, they display a great burst of enthusiasm with lush new growth and bloom. The obvious advantage of growing these plants is that they don't have to be replanted every year, but there are more good reasons to consider them for your landscape. Most perennials require less maintenance than the annual bedding plants, and they also tend to multiply all by themselves giving you a fuller display of plants to share with a friend.

It is a strange phenomenon that when us Yankees move to Florida we tend to forget that trees lose their leaves in the winter and that some plants actually have the audacity to hibernate underground for part of the year. We seem to be offended by plants that want to take a winter vacation. Fortunately for our expectations this climate offers a wealth of perennials that will continue their good work unless a freeze prunes them back to the soil line.

Many of the Florida gardening texts you might read claim there are only a limited number of perennials available for the Florida garden, but this is definitely not the case. There is a wealth of material to be grown in a staggering array of sizes, shapes and shades. There are also a lot of perennials in this state that are at their prime in the winter.

True, you will not find many of the old familiar faces from Detroit or Pittsburgh growing in Orlando or Fort Myers. The summer heat and high humidity take their toll on astilbe, most iris, bleeding hearts, coral bells and perennial phlox while the mild winters don't provide sufficient chill hours for many other Yankee plants like oriental poppies and peonies.

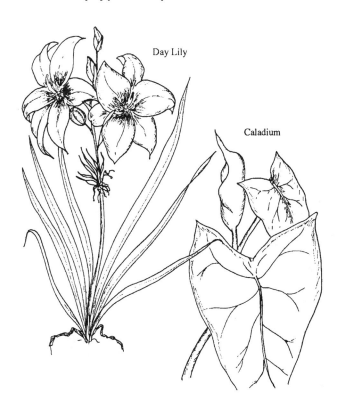

Day Lily

Caladium

FLORIDA PERENNIALS HAVE SEVERAL ADVANTAGES OVER THEIR NORTHERN COUNTERPARTS

Don't be afraid to make some new friend like pentas, bird of paradise, the gingers and so many more.

1. Most Yankee perennials have a blooming season measured in weeks, but many Florida perennials flower for months at a time, some even bloom all year.

2. Florida perennials, if planted properly, require little maintenance.

3. Many Florida perennials make great cut flowers and the more you cut the heavier they bloom.

4. Many of the Florida perennials are inexpensive compared to their northern counterparts.

5. There are perennials for Florida to answer all your landscape needs from ground cover to privacy screen, swamp to sand dune, blistering sun to dense shade.

10 STEPS TO GROWING PERENNIALS IN FLORIDA

1. Plan ahead. Perennials are going to be there for years. Also remember that each species is designed by nature to occupy a certain environment. Planting a bog plant on a sand dune will almost certainly end in failure. Don't fight Mamma Nature, work with her. It's easier and much more successful that way.

2. Contact your local garden club or visit a nearby botanical garden for more information. Your county agricultural extension office and good garden centers can also provide valuable advice before you rush out and grab whatever happens to be on sale this week.

3. Plan for groups of plants, not just one or two of something that caught your eye. Select varieties that compliment each other in size, color, fragrance and blooming season.

4.	Before you plant build a good home for your perennials. Work plenty of compost or organic matter into the soil and work it in deeply. Eighteen inches isn't extreme and twelve inches is a must.

5.	Plant carefully. Avoid setting the plant any deeper in the soil than it was growing in the container. Some plants like gerbera daisies, lisianthus and gazania will do better if you plant so the crown (point where the roots end and the leaves begin) sits on a slight mound, just like you would plant a strawberry.

6.	Don't plant in the heat of the day unless you are a professional landscaper. This can cause stress for both you and your plants. Early morning is a good time to work in the yard; it's cool, the bugs are still asleep and there's no good TV on then.

7.	Water thoroughly and deeply once you have the new arrivals in the ground.

8.	Now is the time to control weeds by using either a pre-emergent herbicide (a chemical that sadistically kills baby weeds just as the seeds begin to sprout) or a porous weed block material over the bed.

9.	It is usually not necessary to fertilize at this time. Give the new plants a couple weeks to make themselves at home, then feed with a balanced slow release fertilizer. If you simply can't bear the thought of putting these plants to bed without a good meal give them a weak solution of one of the liquid fertilizers like Peter's 20-20-20 or Miracle-Gro as a starter solution.

10.	Mulch with decorative stone, bark chips, peanut hulls, cocoa hulls or your favorite mulching material. Then reach for a glass of iced tea and relax.

PERENNIAL BOOK OF LISTS

Based on a poll of growers, landscapers and garden center operators. These are suggestions only and are not intended to be complete lists.

10 BEST ALL AROUND PERENNIALS	
Pentas	Mexican heather
Caladium	Liatris
Society garlic	Gaillardia
Sprengeri fern	Blue daze
Philodendron selloum	Purslane

BEST SUMMER COLOR	BEST WINTER COLOR
Pentas	Gerbera daisy
Gaillardia	Society garlic
Purslane	Verbena
Caladium	Geranium
Liatris	Blue daze

BEST LOW MAINTENANCE	BEST FRAGRANT PERENNIALS
Yucca	Ginger
Gaillardia	Carnation (N & C)
Philodendron selloum	Datura
Liatris	Butterfly weed
Purslane	Four O'Clocks

TOUCH OF HOME OLD FRIENDS	HANG IT UP THEY WON'T GROW IN FLORIDA
Geranium	Virginia bluebells
Hosta	Lily-of-the-valley
Chrysanthemum	Oriental poppy
Shasta daisy	Bleeding heart
Yarrow	Bearded (German) iris

FOR SPECIAL EFFECTS WITH PERENNIALS YOU CAN TRY THESE:

PERENNIAL GROUND COVERS	THE FLORIDA RAIN FOREST
Liriope	Gingers
Sprengeri fern	Banana
Wedelia trilobata	Heliconia
Plumbago	Philodendron selloum
Mexican heather	Ferns
Hottentot fig	Bamboo

THE GREAT FLORIDA DESERT	DOWN BY THE SEA COASTAL PLANTS
Assorted cacti	Wedelia trilobata
Yucca and agave	Hottentot fig
Gaillardia	Gaillardia
Bush daisy	Lantana
Gazania	Crown-of-thorns
Society garlic	Purslane

Pine Cone Ginger

Torch Ginger

GINGERS

Gingers look like the tropics in both foliage and flower. The spice trade may have made the family famous, but they are valuable as easy-to-care-for exotic plants in the Florida landscape. Because there is so much variety you can have different gingers blooming almost all year, in sizes ranging from a few inches to twelve feet. Some have variegated leaves, others have fragrant flowers, all have a certain beauty and mystique about them. With all this going for them you might think they would be frightfully sensitive, extremely difficult to grow and fussier than roses. Not so. They are disgustingly easy.

In general they like a moist soil and do well near a pond or other body of water, but this isn't essential. They do need a soil rich in organic matter and are at their best in full sun or light shade. Most of the gingers are moderately salt tolerant, but don't do well in beach front locations. They respond well to a good balanced fertilizer applied at the beginning of the growing season.

Gingers are grown from tubers and they're offered for sale in most garden centers in the spring, but you will also find many varieties sold as growing plants in containers. if you buy the tubers they should be planted just below the soil surface and covered with a light mulch until growth is under way. After they are actively growing, make certain they're watered during periods of drought and they'll be quite happy.

Gingers form clumps and mats of growth and can easily be divided to increase your display or share with a neighbor. In northern Florida most of the gingers go dormant in the winter, but in frost-free areas most varieties remain green all year. Most of the gingers also make good container plants for your screen room or pool area.

The following are some of the better gingers for the Florida landscape. All are adaptable to any part of the state except areas where there is excessive salt spray or salty water. BUTTERFLY GINGER LILY (Hedychium coronarium) will grow to 6 feet and produce fragrant white flowers throughout the warm months. PINE CONE GINGER (Zingiber zerumbet) produces the red flower cones that are so popular in tropical floral arrangements. The foliage grows to a height of about four feet. They bloom in summer and autumn and go dormant during the shorter days of winter. There is a beautiful variegated form. When the flower cone is handled a strong scent of ginger is released. SHELL GINGER (Alpinia) is available in many varieties ranging from four to eight feet in height. Easy culture and freely produced fragrant flowers make this one of the most popular of the gingers. CURCUMA GINGER LILY (Curcuma inodora) is one of the showiest gingers grown here. Colors range from white to orange and even lavender. This one will grow in almost any soil and will even do well in shady locations. They bloom from mid-summer through autumn. DANCING GIRL GINGER (Globba bulbiferi) is a small ginger maturing at less than two feet, but each new shoot produces a series of yellow blooms. This floral display continues throughout the summer and fall. This is a great ginger for beds and borders or container culture. This one is at its best in light shade and will even thrive on a windowsill. PEACOCK GINGER is a diminutive plant rarely exceeding six or eight inches in height. The almost round foliage is attractive enough to make it a valuable bedding plant, but the lavender flowers in early summer are a bonus. This one is easy in light to medium shade and doesn't care about the soil as long as there is sufficient moisture.

GROWING BULBS IN FLORIDA

If you are a native to anywhere north of Jacksonville you are driven by instinct to practice a series of ancient rituals. First you visit a local garden center and spend hard earned cash for a bag full of ugly brown lumps of something that looks like desiccated onions. As the frosts of the temperate climes force the gardens and gardeners into retreat you bury these dried up blobs, sometimes in intricate patterns and designs. Then magical powders with mystical numbers like 6-12-12 are sprinkled over the entire site.

Is this some primitive religious rite?

No, although it is an expression of faith that spring will come again. This is merely the annual autumnal ritual planting of the spring flowering bulbs. We ALL did it when we lived UP THERE. Remember kneeling in the cool damp earth, trowel in hand, sensing the winter to come, as the dead cold from the soil invaded your body through your knees? If you closed your eyes and the wind was blowing just right through your memories, you could smell the hyacinths and hear the first honeybees as they visit the beautiful beds of tulips that will spring from today's labors.

Toto, we ain't in Kansas anymore; nor are we in Michigan or New Jersey. This is Florida and those great spring bulbs don't do well down here. We know you won't take our word for it, so go ahead and plant these traditions from another climate— just remember "we told you so"!

If the bulbs were pre-chilled or we have an extremely vicious winter you may get some bloom, but the climate that is warm enough to permit swimming in January is so hot by March that a tulip bud will open and shatter in a single day.

We aren't trying to be negative, but there are some things you just don't find in the average Florida backyard, and that list includes both snow shovels and tulips. This is the price we pay for year-round golf and beaches.

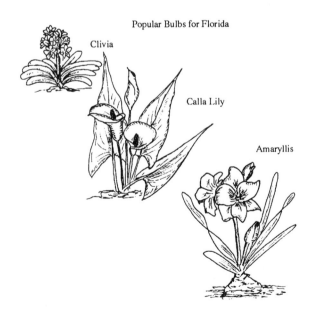

Popular Bulbs for Florida

Clivia

Calla Lily

Amaryllis

TULIPS BY FORCE

You can grow the big three of Dutch enterprise (tulips, hyacinths and narcissus) in Florida, but it takes generous portions of both effort and good luck. These bulbs can be planted in the landscape in extreme north Florida and, while the display will not be as bold nor as long lasting as you experienced in the North, it can still be worth the effort. In central and south Florida, the preparation, planting and maintenance are too great an investment. But if you must have hyacinths don't give up.

It is easier and considerably more rewarding to force these bulbs. Forcing is the process of artificially chilling (to simulate winter), then growing on in containers where you can control the light, moisture and humidity. Once you have met with even limited success at forcing bulbs into bloom you won't ever want to plant a daffodil outdoors again. Forcing gives you total control over when the bloom will open, pests can be almost totally eliminated, weather is immaterial and the flower is beautiful for days rather than hours.

Most of the popular Dutch bulbs like crocus, tulips, hyacinths, Dutch iris and narcissi (note: all daffodils and jonquils are varieties of narcissi) are good candidates for forcing. There are five simple steps to forcing bulbs.

1.   Containers — Select a container that compliments both your decor and pocketbook. Clay, plastic and decorative ceramic planters are available at most garden centers. It is best to use containers with provision for drainage, but you can even use brass pots, vases and other decorative items without drainage holes if you use 2-3 inches of stone chip, marbles or other aggregate in the bottom and are careful with your watering.

2.   Soil — should be light and porous. We have had great success with the "pro-mix" prepared soils and we have also found that a good cactus soil mix works well. You can even grow these bulbs in containers filled with decorative stones, gravel or marbles. For most of the bulbs you will be forcing, 3-6 inches of soil is all they need to put down roots and make a pot a home.

3.   Chilling is necessary for almost all of these spring flowering bulbs. Even the popular paperwhite narcissus will perform better with a few weeks in the cooler, although it isn't necessary to get a

good bloom. You can easily outsmart a flowering bulb and make it think it's been through winter by storing it in the vegetable crisper of your refrigerator for 45 to 60 days. Please note we didn't say freezer. It is best if this chilling process can take place with bulbs already potted up. Remember the old cold frame you used up north? This is because root formation begins during this chilling experience, but since some of you might be reluctant to store potting soil in your fridge, you can compromise and just chill the bulbs in a paper bag.

4.   Potting the bulbs is easy. Small ones like crocus, grape hyacinth and Dutch iris can be pressed into the soil until they are covered by about a quarter inch of the potting medium. The big three are best planted so that the soil comes about two-thirds of the way up the neck of the bulb. After potting it can take from two to ten weeks to develop a strong root system. If you are not chilling the bulbs in the soil then the rooting process should take place in the coolest area of the home you can find. High temperatures speed up the process and an inferior root system is formed.

Don't be afraid to pot up several bulbs in the same container. They can almost be touching each other without causing any harm. They are really quite sociable. We don't recommend mixing species or varieties in the same container, however, because they will not bloom at the same time and you will have buds, blooms and spent plants all in the same pot.

5.   Light is not an important factor while the root system is developing, but as soon as top growth begins the containers should be moved to a sunny windowsill or screen room. Morning sun is better than hot afternoon sun.

The cooler the temperatures the slower the growth of the plant, but the better the appearance will be. By planting containers of bulbs at one or two week intervals, you can keep the colors and scents of a northern spring going much longer.

Once these spring-flowering bulbs have been forced they should be treated like annuals. You enjoyed the fragrance, the colors and memories of springs gone by; now simply discard the spent bulbs. It is almost impossible to rally them for a second year.

BULBS IN THE FLORIDA LANDSCAPE

Don't despair because your backyard isn't blessed with the presence of that brief spring glory you were used to up there. This state offers potential for bulb culture that could only be thought of in terms of windowsill space back in Boston. Think of it — you can grow such exotic plants as amaryllis, clivia, gingers, callas and voodoo lilies in the landscape like you grew daylilies in Detroit.

Another big advantage of Florida gardening is that glads, caladiums and dahlias don't need to be dug and stored for the winter.

Bulbs work into the Florida landscape much the same way you used them as a Yankee. Massed beds are always effective, but borders and containers are also suitable homes for this category of plants.

FIVE TIPS ON GROWING BULBS IN FLORIDA

1.   Most bulbs are at their best in partial shade, but too much shade can produce weak spindly growth, poor quality bloom or attract insects and disease.

2.   Most bulbs respond best to a well drained site, but consult the ready reference lists that follow for details, because many Florida bulbs even thrive in bog conditions.

3.   Before planting work plenty of organic matter into the existing soil to a depth of at least 8-12 inches.

4.   You can mix a good bulb fertilizer into the soil before planting. Many experts recommend using super-phosphate as an additive, but it is essential to use a complete fertilizer formula (one that provides nitrogen, phosphorous and potassium) in Florida's less than rich sandy soil. A well-balanced meal is important for bulb-type plants too.

5.   Consult your local agricultural extension office, local garden club or garden center for details on specific plants and their cultivation.

The following lists are only suggestions and this is by no means a complete catalog of the thousands of plants grown from bulbs, tubers, corms, etc. that will give you good results in Florida.

OLD FRIENDS FROM THE NORTH COUNTRY THAT WILL GROW HERE

Allium
Calla lily
Canna
Cyclamen
Dahlia
Freesia
Fritillaria
Gladiolus
Gloxinia
Lilies
Oxalis
Tuberous begonia
Daylily

OLD FRIENDS FROM THE NORTH THAT WON'T GROW WELL HERE

Bearded iris
Dutch (bulb) iris
Crocus
Grape hyacinth
Hyacinth
Narcissus
Japanese iris
Scilla
Tulip
Lily-of-the-valley

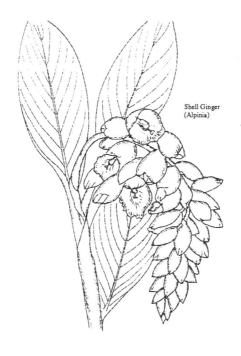

Shell Ginger
(Alpinia)

TOP TEN BULBS FOR FLORIDA — Nominated by garden center and landscaping professionals.

Agapanthus (Lily-of-the-Nile or African lily) — Beautiful blue or white flower heads; rugged plant for landscape.

Amaryllis (Hippeastrum) can be forced for holiday bloom or grown in containers, flower beds, borders and accent groupings.

Blood lily (Haemanthus) — Rich red globes of bloom followed by tropical looking foliage.

Caladiums are grown commercially in Central Florida. Extremely versatile plant for massed beds, edgings or containers.

Cannas are sinfully easy in Florida. They give bright colored bloom and tropical looking foliage in spite of those ugly green caterpillars.

Clivia — Boldly orange with a tropical appearance, but the big plus is that it is almost trouble free.

Crinum lilies can be massive, are rugged and have a carefree tropical appearance.

Daylilies are a favorite everywhere. By planting carefully selected varieties you can have daylilies blooming throughout the warm months.

Shell ginger is one of the most widely planted gingers because it blooms throughout the warm months and the flowers are fragrant.

Zepheranthus (rain lily, fairy lily) is a pint size version of the amaryllis and is magnificent in massed plantings.

BULBS FOR WET AREAS	
Canna	African iris
Elephant ears	Louisiana iris
Gingers	Spiral flag

HOW WELL DO YOU KNOW YOUR BULBS, TUBERS AND CORMS?

Try this little quiz on what's happening in the underground culture of Florida bulbs.

1. Bulbs should have their foliage cut back after blooming.　　T　F

2. We call them all bulbs, but only the lilies have true bulbs. Everything else is a tuber.　　T　F

3. African iris (Moraea) is ever blooming in frost-free areas.　　T　F

4. The gloriosa lily bulb is poisonous.　　T　F

5. Garlic and onions are flowering bulbs.　　T　F

6. Tuberoses, known for their fragrance, bloom in mid-winter in Florida.　　T　F

7. The shell ginger isn't a ginger at all, it is a member of the banana family.　　T　F

8. Gladiolus will bloom continuously in Florida.　　T　F

9. Dahlias won't grow in Florida.　　T　F

10. Cannas are so versatile they will grow in both bogs and dry upland areas.　　T　F

Florida natives know there are three ways to tell if your new neighbor is a Yankee transplant. If you look at his yard and see a staghorn fern hanging from the carport it's a good possibility you've got a newcomer. If there is also a newly planted orange tree in the front yard you can be almost certain. If there is a plastic flamingo beside the orange tree you can be positive.

SECTION TWO

THE TARZAN COMPLEX

Native Floridians joke about the three ways you can tell if the new neighbor is a recently transplanted Yankee. The new arrival is the one with the plastic pink flamingo along the path, staghorn ferns hanging from the live oaks and a newly planted orange in the front yard.

All right, let them laugh. We served our time shoveling snow and staring at naked trees for months on end. We came here seeking a tropical paradise and we have a right to remodel our own personal sand pile into whatever we want.

A tropical effect isn't all that difficult to achieve in north or central Florida. In the southern end of the state the problem is how to keep this paradise from growing over the driveway or crawling through the windows.

Let's try an experiment. Close your eyes for a few minutes and think about the perfect island paradise. What do you see? Does dense jungle growth laden with masses of bright fragrant flowers come to mind? Or do you see swaying palms and sunny skies? Either way, in Florida it is within your grasp, and it won't take too much effort either.

There is a wealth of tropical looking plant material that is fully hardy or requires little protection to survive the stress of a north Florida winter. You can combine crape myrtle, rugged palms and loquats with gingers and elephant ears, then by adding a few ferns and potted flowering plants you have created your own private jungle. Looks steamy tropical, but only your landscaper knows for sure.

Central Florida opens the backyard to much more of the tropics. Exotic tree ferns, sago palms, bougainvillea and bird-of-paradise require some winter protection, but generally thrive from Orlando south. Crotons, powderpuffs and hibiscus are only a few of the plants that will freeze to the ground during a severe cold spell, but this is merely frost pruning and most will bounce back with enthusiasm.

South Florida is almost as tropical as the Caribbean islands and the potential for exotic plant growth is almost unlimited. Your landscape can be home to fragrant frangi-pani (plumeria), African tulip trees, tender eucalyptus and the old friend from the corner of your northern dining room, the rubber tree (ficus elastica). Rex begonias are used as bedding plants while coconuts and mangos are dooryard fruit.

LAWS OF THE JUNGLE

The greatest problem for the newcomer to Florida isn't finding plant material that they can use in their backyard jungle. No, the biggest problem is knowing when to stop planting.

1.   Remember, what you plant will grow up, and since the growing season is months longer, plant material matures faster. A tropical looking jacaranda that you brought home in a three gallon pot will, in a few short years, be over forty feet tall and cover the entire front yard.

2.   The closer the plants grow to each other the greater the chances for disease, insect problems and all those creepy crawly things that send you back to the safety and comfort of the living room.

3.   The greater the number of plants you have in your personal paradise the more labor intensive it becomes.

4.   No matter how mild the past winter was, sooner or later the frost will come. So will the drought. An unmanageable number of tender plants, trees and shrubs that need to be moved, covered or otherwise protected can only bring exhaustion, despair and mourning over lost botanical treasures.

5.   Some of these tropical plants are like teenagers, they're difficult to control. Your neighbors may resent the beautiful bamboo from your backyard spreading into their lawn, vines like pandora and passion vine assume the neighbor's fence is theirs to cover and lawn beyond theirs to claim.

You left some magnificent trees and shrubs to brave the northern winters alone when you headed south. White paper birch, blue spruce, crimson king maples, lilacs and forsythia are only a few of the old friends that you will be replacing with orange trees, palms, hibiscus and all that stuff you used to grow on your windowsill. The following are some lists of suggestions for your exotic paradise. These are only the tip of the tropical iceberg so to speak.

COLD HARDY PLANTS WITH TROPICAL APPEARANCE FOR NORTH FLORIDA	
Bamboo varieties	Bananas and hibiscus
Crape myrtles	Many ferns
Cabbage, rhapis & pindo palms	Cyperus
Loquats	Gingers
Dwarf poinciana	Caladiums and elephant ears

TROPICAL LOOKING PLANTS THAT MAY BE FROST PRUNED IN NORTH AND CENTRAL FLORIDA	
Allamanda and mandevilla	Gingers
Amaryllis	Some varieties of ferns
Hibiscus in a multitude of ever blooming varieties	Citrus (some varieties are hardier than others)
Hong Kong orchid tree Bauhinia	Powderpuff, both red and dwarf pink
Pentas	Datura

VINES FOR TROPICAL EFFECT IN BACKYARD JUNGLE

1. Bougainvillea (really a sprawling shrub)
2. Passion vine (dozens of great varieties to choose from)
3. Pandora vine (great from central Florida south)
4. Chalice vine (spectacular, but tender)
5. Beaumontia (another truly tropical vine)
6. Wisteria (the old standard is at its best in north Florida)

TROPICAL FRUIT FOR YOUR JUNGLE

1. Wherever you live in Florida there is a fragrant flowering citrus for you. Even if it has to live in a portable container.
2. Loquats lend a tropical grace to any site.
3. Bananas come in a variety of sizes. All have a ragged informality.
4. Natal plum combines fragrant flowers, delicious fruit and a tolerance for drought and salt.
5. Pineapple (at one time a commercial crop in Florida)
6. Mango (central and south)
7. Avocado (central and south)
8. Cassava (tapioca source)

There is a little more information on tropical fruit in the chapter on oranges. Don't hesitate to contact your agricultural extension office, plant societies or local library for details and specifics.

Banana

ORCHIDS

Orchids can easily become a part of your own botanical Eden in Florida. Whether you hang them in the oak trees in the backyard and ignore them or pamper them on the Florida room they will usually reward you with the most exotic of bloom.

Some orchids are epyphitic (like Spanish moss and other bromeliads) and will happily grow in trees or hanging baskets filled with bark. Others are terrestrial (like the lady's slipper) and need to put down roots in the soil. Either way they aren't nearly as fussy as most folks think. Most of the exotic varieties are cold sensitive so they may need some winter protection in the central and northern parts of the state.

CATTLEYA orchids are magnificent, the bloom is long-lasting and there are hundreds of varieties that are suitable for the beginner or serious grower.

CYPRIPEDIUM (the lady's slipper) is a terrestrial orchid that can be found growing in moist forested areas over much of the country. Many varieties are available from nurseries and garden centers. Don't try to collect them from the wild. Your chances of successfully transplanting them are almost nil and it is against the law in most areas.

VANILLA is harvested from the beans of Vanilla fragrans, one of the few vining orchids. It is also one of the few edible orchids. While the greenish flower isn't as striking as a cattleya it is not overly difficult to grow and does well in south Florida.

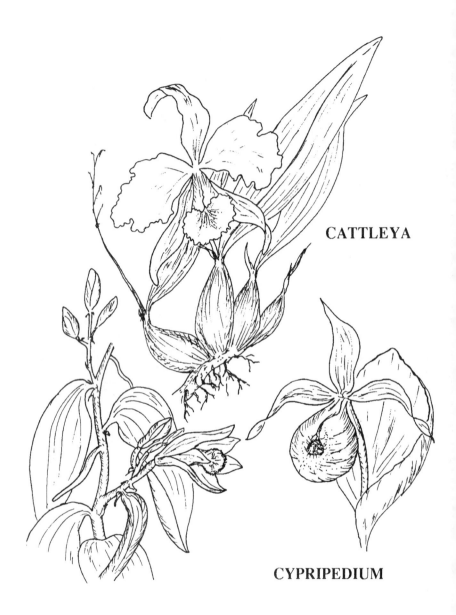

CATTLEYA

CYPRIPEDIUM

VANILLA

Hong Kong
Orchid Tree

Bauhinia, several species in white, pink, purple and brick red

THE PORTABLE LANDSCAPE, CONTAINER CULTURE

Some of the plants you have always wanted to grow in your personal jungle are either very cold sensitive or unsuited to Florida soils. Don't let that discourage you. You can keep them quite happy in containers. The bigger pots you may want to keep on dollies so that they can be easily moved.

Container growing offers a number of advantages over permanent homes in the soil.

1. Easy to protect from cold weather. You can pick it up and put it in the garage.

2. Changing landscape features is easier than moving the living room furniture.

3. It's easy to pull a blooming tree or shrub to a highly visible location. One of our friends has what he refers to as his "bragging spot" and there by the front entrance you will find the best the season has to offer.

4. In a container growth can be controlled. Aggressive Saddam Hussein types like bamboo and cyperus won't be as likely to invade their neighbors. Trees can more easily be kept shrub size and in some cases bloom can be encouraged.

5. It is easier to control many pests like nematodes when the plant is in a container.

6. As the plants grow they can be turned, repositioned, spaced further apart or moved from one part of the landscape to another when you change your mind.

If you choose to create a portable jungle you might want to keep the following suggestions in mind:

1. Use containers that have proper drainage provision. We mean holes in the bottom so that water doesn't stand in the pot. Unless they are aquatic plants the roots can drown if the soil is saturated for several consecutive days.

2.   Use a loose soil rich in organic matter. Your plants can't climb out for a snack when they get hungry. It will be up to you to provide what they need.

3.   Water frequently. A drip irrigation system is easy and uses a lot less water.

4.   Feed regularly but not too heavily.

5.   A large pot housing a tree or shrub can serve double duty. Plant smaller foliage, flowering material or vines that can serve as a ground cover. Not only will this soften the look of pot and bare soil, it will conserve moisture and double the number of plants you can grow in a limited amount of space.

THE DINNER TABLE JUNGLE

You can purchase tropical plants at the local garden center, swap cuttings with neighbors, join an active garden club or plant some of the table scraps. Go ahead and laugh, but after you've made guacamole from the avocado what are you going to do with the seed? What about the seeds from papayas, mangos and pomegranates, or the peelings from sweet potatoes? It's so simple and easy. Stick the seeds in a pot filled with good soil, keep watered and, while you're waiting, finish reading this book. Okay, so they may not be the named varieties, they still quickly grow into tropical looking plants that might even flower and some will bear fruit. We have started a lot of our own personal jungle with seeds rescued from the dinner table, botanical gardens and roadside.

Some of the tropical produce you can find at the local supermarket can be started from tubers or cuttings. Yams and sweet potatoes grow with reckless abandon and make an excellent ground cover if you have a large area available. Taro, dasheen and yautia are all root crops that grow rapidly into impressive tropical foliage and you can start them from small whole tubers found at the produce counter. Cassava is another tropical plant that the neighbors might think is marijuana, but in reality it is the source of tapioca and forms a striking seven foot tall perennial plant. For more information on these see the chapter on vegetable gardening.

43

THE CARE AND FEEDING OF A JUNGLE

Okay, Tarzan, now you have swaying palms and tropical fruit trees surrounding the pool and the backyard has been replaced with a thatched cabana and bar. You've got your jungle, now what are you going to do with it? The following are some suggestions on how to make easy maintenance a reality.

- Prune, trim and weed frequently. This is easier on both the plants and you.

- Use drip irrigation where possible. It is inexpensive to install and efficient to operate.

- Use mulches, weed block fabric and edging barriers to cut down on the growth of unwanted vegetation that wants to be a part of your paradise.

- Watch containerized plants for adventurous roots that want to crawl out and go exploring. Trim them off before they become a major problem. Turning the pots periodically will discourage this and also create a more balanced plant.

- Use a slow release fertilizer like Osmocote for more controlled growth and less effort on your part.

- Keep fallen leaves and debris gathered and add this to the compost pile. This will also help control disease and undesirable pests.

- Remember that these plants, even the seedlings, will grow. Plan and plant for mature sizes. This is another reason for container growing at least some of your exotics. They can be easily thinned when growth demands.

- Keep material spaced far enough apart that air can circulate. This promotes strong healthy growth and helps prevent disease.

- Don't panic at the sight of an insect. Most are beneficial and many of the rest aren't a threat unless the population runs wild. Bugs are simply a part of the natural order of things.

- You can probably use some outside help to control the pests mentioned above. Bird houses and bird feeders will attract efficient yet inexpensive controls. They are willing to set up housekeeping in your paradise if you can keep the neighborhood cats and squirrels under control. Not only are the birds the cheapest insect control you can hire, they are environmentally safe and besides, they're more fun to watch than a tank sprayer.

PALMS MEAN PARADISE

Let's face it, palms look tropical. That's why they are such an important part of the Florida landscape. Warning: Pay attention. There will be a quiz later.

It doesn't matter whether it is commercial or residential, professional or homeowner planned, palms fit into the Florida lifestyle. There are a number of good reasons why you might want to consider this group of plants in your landscape.

1. Because many of them are native to the state, they know how to survive.

2. There is a great deal of variety in size, leaf form and color. Thus, they can answer a multitude of landscaping needs.

3. Smaller growing varieties are great in containers, as accents or understory plants in semi-shady areas.

4. Palms have few serious pests, and they require little maintenance.

5. They aren't fussy about soil type as long as they get a proper feeding program.

There are many varieties of palms to be found garden centers all over this state including the majestic state tree, the sabal palm. Some palms form clumps (multiple trunks) while other species produce only a solitary trunk. When you are palm shopping some Saturday morning there are several factors to take into consideration.

1. How big will it grow? It doesn't matter how big it is in a three gallon pot. What is it going to look like in ten years? Will it tower over the house or will it be a pleasant focal point for the pool area?

2. Is it cold hardy? If not, are you prepared to keep it in a container, provide frost protection or take the chance of losing it?

45

3. How fast does it grow? If it is a slow growing variety you might want to buy a larger specimen, rather than wait years for it to become what you expect it to be.

4. Are there disease or insect problems that you would be wise to avoid. Lethal yellows, as an example, is a fatal disease of coconut palms.

5. If you get a large specimen palm do you want to use a professional planting service or try to plant and brace it yourself? Large palms are moved with little root structure. Until a new anchoring system is in place, they are at the mercy of the wind unless properly supported.

Cabbage Palm
(Sabal palmetto)

PLANTING PALMS IN YOUR LANDSCAPE

You are most likely to select container grown palms that can be found in most independent and chain garden centers. These are the easiest to transport and plant. They also experience little transplanting shock and can be added to your backyard almost any time of the year without fear of loss.

Palms are quite tolerant of soil type and thrive in our Florida sand. It won't hurt to add some organic matter however. It is also a good idea to make a collar of soil a couple feet in circumference to serve as a water reservoir. This will keep the water near the roots while it soaks into the soil rather than running off toward the driveway. This is a good idea for almost all trees and shrubs you plant here. It is generally good practice to water newly planted palms well about three times a week.

Palms can take full sun, but most will also willingly accept partial shade, particularly the lower growing species.

After planting feed with a good balanced plant food. Follow the directions on the bag and don't overdo it.

Palms respond well to a complete food that contains sufficient iron and magnesium. The following is a schedule that works well.

1st feeding — in February or March

2nd feeding — in June or July

3rd feeding — in September or October.

This application can help prevent cold damage, but given too late it can encourage unseasonable growth that is more susceptible to freezing.

WARNING: THIS IS A TEST

We warned you that there would be a quiz at the end of the chapter. Now, let's see how well you know Florida palms?

1. Honey produced from the flowers of the native cabbage palm is poisonous. T F

2. The trunks of some date palms can be tapped like maple trees in the north to obtain a sugar rich sap. T F

3. Native Americans in Florida ate the hearts of certain palms. Early European settlers tried it and thought it tasted like cabbage. That's why we call it the cabbage palm. T F

4. When a coconut is ripe there is no "milk" in it. T F

5. There is a palm grown in Florida that has needle like spines. T F

6. Palms need salt laden soil to grow well and if you live in the center of the state you will need to add special salt enriched fertilizers. T F

7. Rattan furniture is made from a vining palm that may reach several hundred feet in length. T F

8. When the heart of a royal palm trunk is damaged or removed the palm will produce branches. T F

9. There are male and female date trees and one male is planted in a grove of females to provide pollen. T F

10. Bamboo is a type of palm that forms clumps rather than a solitary trunk. T F

WHAT'S LURKING IN YOUR BACKYARD JUNGLE?

Snakes are a fact of life in Florida, and down here they don't hibernate during winter. Most snakes aren't dangerous and pose no threat to you. In fact, they feed on insects, small rodents, frogs, lizards, other snakes and, unfortunately, sometimes bird eggs and baby birds, but, hey, it's a jungle out there!

This state does have some poisonous snakes including several rattlesnakes, the famous cottonmouth and, of course, the colorful coral snake. We recommend that you consult the Winner Publications wildlife series titles on Florida snakes to make yourself an expert.

If you live near a lake (most folks in Florida do), swamp or large mud puddle you may be visited by the closest thing we've got to a dinosaur, the alligator. Folks think it's really cute to feed wild gators, but this is really dumb. For one thing they may view your poodle or pet tabby as lunch and if you have taught them not to fear mankind, small children might even look like dinner.

We guarantee you will see multitudes of lizards, skinks, frogs, toads and salamanders. This brings us to a strange and fascinating quirk in the Florida language. What they call a salamander Yankees call a gopher. But to true Florida crackers a gopher is a tortoise. Incidentally, the term "cracker" comes from the crack of the whip used by the Florida cowboys on their cattle drives. This state has a rich history of ranching and beef production exceeds many western states even today.

The anole is a small native lizard that can change colors to blend in with whatever piece of living room furniture it happens to be sitting on. For this reason it is sometimes referred to as a chameleon, but true chameleons are found mainly in pet stores. Some folks become hyper when one of our little lizards is spotted in the house but relax, they are harmless, that is unless you are a bug like a cockroach.

Don't feed the squirrels. You think they are cute, don't you? Picture a squirrel without that fuzzy tail and what do you have? A rat. Squirrels raid bird feeders, dine on bird eggs, will wreak havoc on your garden, rip the buds and blooms from everything from camellias and guavas to passion vines. Suggestion: encourage your neighbor to feed them. Then watch as they rip his screen room to shreds to get at the barbecue grill.

Armadillos are among our favorite animals. I know they can tear divots out of the lawn, but they only do that when they are dining on ants. Yes, they even eat fire ants. Armadillos have been moving east and north for most of this century and, along with the coyote, are mother nature's way of telling us who's really in charge. Incidentally, if you live in north or central Florida you might catch a glimpse of a coyote too.

Raccoons and opossums will also frequent your backyard in Florida and they will boldly come up to the door and demand a handout. They can also do considerable harm to your vegetable garden. Because raccoons can carry rabies we do recommend caution when dealing with them. In most areas Animal Control will set live traps and move them to a neighbor's yard for you.

With Florida wildlife, like life in general, it's the little things that really bother you the most. Little things like mosquitoes, fire ants, scorpions, black widow spiders, the dreaded brown recluse spider and several poisonous caterpillars. Notice we didn't even mention the hornets, yellow jackets, wasps and their venomous kin.

Have we scared you off yet? Have courage and take heart. Mosquitoes can be controlled by eliminating their breeding sites, like standing and stagnant water. Where that isn't possible spraying the waterways with BT (that's Bacillus thuringiensis, a natural control that is only harmful to caterpillars, mosquito larva and a few other bugs) limits the population. The lizards, frogs and small snakes view many of these venomous creatures as a gourmet meal. Bats, purple martins, flycatchers and dozens of other birds will eat their weight in mosquitoes, gnats and other buzzing beasts.

Proper maintenance also helps to keep these critters in check. Then you have to worry about the ones that attack your plants like slugs, white fly, mites and aphids; but that's another story.

GOING NATIVE

Anytime two people meet in Florida, early in the conversation the question will be asked, "And where are you from?" Florida, for most of us, is a destination. Born and bred natives are at least a minority if not a rarity. Look around your neighborhood and you will probably find more folks born in states north of here or even places beyond our shores than can claim to be of Florida stock. Your landscape is also a United Nations of plants with camellias from Japan, poinsettias from Mexico and pyracanthas from Europe.

Logic tells us there must have been a lot of spectacular plants growing here when the European explorers first found these beaches or they wouldn't have called it Florida. There are a good many of these natives that grace your backyard and ours. Live and Laurel oaks, sabal palms, red maples, several pines, magnolias and loblolly bays are only a few of the natives that are valuable members of the backyard community. They are often overlooked because they are common, or mundane or not tropical enough. But they have had thousands of years of experience coping with the climate, soil and insects that are also a part of life here.

We see red maple and sweet gum in the north and central parts of the state and they don't look tropical. We think the natives are weeds and want to use something more exotic. We have watched newcomers rip out beautiful mature oaks and pines so that they can plant saplings of cold sensitive eucalyptus and tender palms or labor intensive roses. The native trees, shrubs and even many of the vines are eager to be valuable contributing members of your landscape. A weed is best described as "any plant growing where it isn't wanted." To Mama Nature there are no weeds, unless it would be roses, corn and some of the other plants that have been so hybridized that they can't even survive without your help. Don't be too quick to disparage these natives because they are common. They deserve a place in your landscape.

WHY USE NATIVE PLANTS?

1.   As we mentioned above they are survivors and know how to cope with insects, drought and even nematodes.

2.   In a state that is surrounded by salt water we are forced to turn to the natives to get some green growing on the coastal areas where salt tolerance is necessary.

3.   They look like the real Florida, complete with the Spanish moss and tillandsias, beauty berry and swamp hibiscus, elderberry and Chickasaw plum.

4.   The native plants attract birds, butterflies and other wildlife.

5.   It makes environmental sense to propagate and use some of Florida's endangered species in the landscape.

WHERE TO FIND NATIVE TREES, SHRUBS AND PLANTS

Now that we have convinced you that you need to know where to find these plants. The first and obvious answer would be "in the woods." There is a problem there though. If it's private property you may find that you've upset another variety of Florida native, and this one carries a shotgun. You are trespassing and digging plants growing on someone else's property is theft. Unless you want to lounge around in a government operated condo with bars on the windows don't, we repeat, DON'T collect plant materials from a state or national park. They take this seriously and so should everyone else. Those parks are for the benefit and enjoyment of everyone. Don't be cheap, selfish or a thief.

If you do want to collect plants from the wild you might want to contact those in charge of clearing road cuts and development areas. They will often grant permission if asked, but can get seriously agitated when you don't say please. These clearing sites are a good source for small trees, shrubs, wildflowers, ferns, mosses and much more, but care must be exercised if the transplants are to survive.

Here are a few suggestions to help:

1. Don't try to move too large a plant, tree or shrub. In this sandy soil the roots have to spread far and deep for moisture and nutrients. You are going to do serious damage when you dig (never pull or rip the plant from the ground).

2. Wrap the soil and root mass in burlap, plastic or put it in a pot or nursery can as soon as you dig it.

3. Keep the roots from drying out and replant it as soon as possible.

4. Take note of the type of soil and area where the plant was growing and don't move it if you can't give it a new home somewhat like that. A bog plant won't do well in your dry backyard, no matter how beautiful the leaves are. If it was growing in full sun the shady corner by the fence won't be appreciated.

5. Prune back the top twenty-five percent of most trees and shrubs to compensate for the root damage.

6. Keep well watered through the first season.

7. Give a light feeding with a starter solution, but avoid high nitrogen fertilizers until the transplants are well established.

8. Remember that many native plants are very demanding as to soil, pH, moisture, light, etc. Unless you have put serious study into this mistakes are going to be made. If you want to learn more about the specific needs of native plants, contact the environmental organizations like the Florida Native Plant Society or the Audubon Society.

9. Don't take more than you can plant and care for.

10. Remember that native plants harvested from the wild don't have a good survival rate under the best of conditions. If half of what you collect make it through the first year rejoice.

Digging native plants from the wild is work and success is often doubtful, but there are better ways to get native plants into your landscape. Most nurseries are now growing and selling many of these trees and shrubs. There are clubs and organizations that trade and sell native plants. One other suggestion we can make is to collect seeds and take cuttings to start new plants. It may take a little longer, but with the lengthy growing season a seedling may catch up with a five foot sapling you transplanted.

The following are some native Floridians you might want to invite into your backyard. We have used N, C & S to designate recommended areas of Florida where these plants will grow the best. With extra care you will very likely be able to grow many of these beyond the ideal zones.

NATIVE TREES FOR SHADE

Bald cypress	NC
Live oak	NCS
Laurel oak	NCS
Red maple	NCS
Gumbo-limbo	S
Sand pine	NCS
Slash pine	NCS
Sweet gum	NCS
Cabbage palm	NCS
Florida boxwood	S

FLOWERING NATIVE TREES

Chickasaw plum	NC	white flowers in spring
Cinnamon-bark	S	purple flowers in fall
Flowering dogwood	NC	white flowers in spring
Geiger tree	S	orange flowers all year
Lignum-vitae	S	blue flowers in spring
Mahoe	S	yellow flowers all year
Redbud	NC	pink or purple flowers in spring
Yaupon holly	NC	many hollies throughout state
Loblolly bay	NCS	white flowers during warm months
Southern magnolia	NC	white flowers spring to early summer

NATIVE SHRUBS FOR FLOWERS

Swamp hibiscus	CS	pink and red bloom; warm months
Golden dewdrop	CS	blue flowers, yellow fruit, warm months
Spanish bayonet	NCS	several yucca varieties, white bloom in spring
Eastern coralbean (Cherokee bean)	NCS	red flowers in spring, red seeds in fall
Firebush	NCS	red flowers in fall

NATIVE SHRUBS TO ATTRACT BIRDS

American beautyberry	NC	lavender flowers in spring, purple berries in fall and winter
Blueberry	NC	several native varieties birds love
Gallberry	NCS	one of several native hollies birds enjoy
Wax myrtle	NCS	southern version of bayberry
Cocoplum	CS	a twenty foot shrub that serves double duty as a hedge

BUTTERFLIES IN THE GARDEN

Florida is home to about 160 species of butterflies and over three thousand native plants that feed them. There are also hundreds of landscape plants that serve as fodder for the butterflies that haven't earned their wings yet. Yes, those caterpillars that were devouring your croton leaves yesterday will be tomorrow's winged beauties. Fortunately most of the young prefer the wild flowers we usually call weeds but even if they munch a few leaves from the landscape its only nature's way of pruning and isn't it a small price to pay for the little specks of rainbow in flight?

The butterfly kids like to munch on the following:

Almost all citrus	Butterfly weed
Crotons	Fetterbush
Hosta	Milkweed
Oaks	Thistles
Willow	

Almost every weed has a caterpillar that thinks its delicious. Winged caterpillars (adult butterflies) feed on the nectar of many flowers and in the process are important in the pollination of many plants, second only to the common honey bee.

The following are a few of the plants adults visit for dinner:

Acacias	All citrus	Bottlebrush
Bougainvillea	Buddleia	Butterfly weed
Calendula	Cassias	Clover
Coreopsis	Gallardia	Gazania
Honeysuckle	Impatiens	Lantana
Liatris	Marigolds	Mints
Pentas	Salvia	Verbena
Zinnia		

An easy addition to your butterfly garden is a six inch clay saucer filled with fresh water. They do get thirsty and on a hot afternoon will mass at a water station.

One word of caution if you are trying to attract butterflies. The bug sprays have to go. Butterflies are insects and both the larvae and the adults are easily killed by almost all the commonly used insecticides.

HUMMINGBIRDS

Only one species of hummingbird is commonly seen in Florida, the ruby-throat. It is plentiful and will eagerly visit a feeding station. We aren't referring to the plastic hummingbird feeders that one of our friends referred to as a McDonald's for midget birds with a drinking problem. The feeding station that is the most fun for both you and the hummingbirds, is a part of your garden they can call their own, filled with the stuff they love to eat. Hummingbirds are a lot like raging bulls in that they are both attracted by the color red. Red flowers filled with nectar are like a magnet to these little charmers. You may be interested to know that these birds don't limit their diet to syrupy liquids, they also relish small insects and spiders. They will even rob spider webs of the snacks the hard working spider collected.

Among the many plants that hummingbirds frequent are:

Honeysuckle	Four-O'Clock
Trumpet creeper	Geiger tree (South Florida)
Coral bean	Firebush (Hamelia patens)
Cross vine	Hibiscus
Powderpuff	Red buckeye (North Florida)
Nicotiana	Many other annuals, perennials and herbs

SECTION THREE

THE FLORIDA LAWN, ANOTHER GREEN MYTH

SAY GOOD-BYE TO KENTUCKY BLUE GRASS

If your ultimate gardening fantasy is a lush expanse of deep green lawn then you are in the wrong state. We don't mean to alarm you but, aside from some theme parks where they must spend all their after hours time replacing the sod, turf is the most difficult part of your home landscape to establish and maintain. It's not impossible; let's just say it's a challenge.

True, there are some grasses that can give an irregular pattern of green to your yard wide sand pile, but don't expect to find that soft even texture of bluegrass or fescue that you left behind with the snow. No, what we have for turf here more closely resembles crabgrass and orchard weeds. Up north you could build a lawn by simply throwing out a handful of seeds on some warm April weekend. It's not quite that easy in Florida.

We don't want to discourage you about the prospects of owning a Florida lawn you can be proud to show to your Yankee friends and relatives, and if mowing is your favorite exercise there will still be plenty of opportunity. First, let's take a look at your options.

SEVEN CHOICES FOR FLORIDA TURF

1.   ST. AUGUSTINE GRASS can give you a rich green dense turf that looks somewhat like well behaved crabgrass. It is the turf of choice in central and coastal areas of our state because it has good salt and shade tolerance. There are many varieties available, but beware because some of them are wimpy when it comes to a little cold weather and almost all of them are the favorite food of chinch bugs.

2.   BAHIA was originally brought into this country from Brazil as an orchard grass on our sorry excuse for soil. It may not be the prettiest of grasses, but it has one big advantage. It grows well from seed and that makes it relatively inexpensive to establish. There are other advantages too.

Once established it will defiantly stand up to heat, drought and the pounding traffic from herds of kids. The down side of Bahia is it's open growth habit and the fact that it enthusiastically produces tall seed heads, sometimes only a day or two after mowing. They also have a coarse texture, low salt tolerance and an irresistible appeal to mole crickets.

Bahia comes in two basic varieties. Argentine Bahia grows denser and has a richer color so it makes a better lawn. Pensacola Bahia is a rugged individualist with fewer maintenance needs and is most often used for playgrounds and road cuts.

3.   CENTIPEDE GRASS is the lawn of choice for most of northern Florida and the Panhandle, but it is well suited to the central part of the state as well. It spreads quickly with good tolerance for shade and drought. Unfortunately, it is very susceptible to nematodes and is a little sensitive to foot traffic.

4.   CARPET GRASS is a low-growing, reasonably dense creeping grass from the Caribbean that has a liking for wet soils where all of the above suffer. It also tolerates semi-shady areas well. Unfortunately, it is shallow rooted and does not survive drought or dry soils. It also goes dormant early and greens up late.

5.   BERMUDA GRASS demands the greatest maintenance and provides the highest quality. It's the grass of choice for Florida golf course greens.

Here is a turf that grows rapidly, producing fine textured, dense, deep green lawns that have good salt tolerance. Bermuda doesn't do well in shade and while there are few disease problems nematodes and a wide range of insects consider it a delicacy. For best effect it needs frequent (every 3-7 days) close mowing with a reel type mower, almost daily watering and more fertilizer than most other grasses.

6.   ANNUAL RYE is an old friend from the great Northern lawns. Up there you used it as a cover or nurse grass while the bluegrass and fescue were germinating and becoming established. Down here it's a winter grass. Because most of the turf grasses popular in Florida don't grow much in the cool months when it's somewhat more pleasant to actually get out in the yard and push a lawnmower we plant annual rye. The rye provides instant green while our permanent turf is dormant or inactive.

Annual rye will thrive through the cooler winter season, but withers quickly in the late spring heat and humidity. Incidentally, unlike in the northern states, perennial rye is strictly a winter season grass giving you only a few months of green not a couple years.

7.   TALL FESCUE is another old friend that you may remember from the snow states. It's planted in the northern and north central sections of Florida as a pasture or playground grass, but while it has some shade tolerance it simply can't take the Florida heat farther south. It grows quickly from seed and has some drought tolerance, but isn't grown frequently because there are better options for the lawn.

WHY LAWNS ARE DIFFICULT IN FLORIDA

Accept it as a fact of life, "A lush green lawn is the most difficult part of your landscape in Florida." There are several reasons for this.

Heading the list would have to be the fact that Mamma Nature didn't even try to plant a turf type grass in this state. We put ourselves in direct opposition to the forces of nature when we plant a yard full of this green stuff. Mamma nature would rather grow oak trees, beauty berry, spiderworts, thistles and several hundred other wildflowers we call weeds. They were here first and have had millennia of experience dealing with the heat and humidity, not to mention the bugs.

Much of this state is caught in this nether-land between temperate and tropical climates where the winters are too cold for some grasses and the summers are too hot for others. Our sandy soil holds water like a sieve and is home to enormous populations of nematodes. If we water the beautiful grasses enough to keep them green we encourage fungus disease. Then, of course, there are the mole crickets (the world's number one ugliest insect), chinch bugs, sod webworms, army worms and a multitude of other insects that think you planted the lawn just for them.

As if this isn't enough there are squirrels that delight in burying and then reclaiming acorns and other little tidbits. And they never bother to replace the divots. Armadillos will gleefully turn ant hills inside out while dining on their favorite snack. While this is beneficial it still creates aesthetic problems for your lawn.

If you aren't thoroughly discouraged then you are probably courageous enough to forge ahead and establish a Florida lawn. It isn't impossible, and if you plan ahead and prepare well your chances of success are good.

SOD, SEED OR PLUGS?

You have at least three choices when it comes to establishing a lawn, whether it is from bare soil or a renovation project.

1.   SOD is, naturally, the quickest way to create a finished lawn. This is generally the most expensive, however, and it is back-breaking work. After laying a pallet of sod you will have a good deal of respect for those folks that do it for a living. You can find St. Augustine, Bahia and Bermuda sod readily, but for some of the other common grasses you may have to turn to seed.

2.   PLUGS of many St. Augustine varieties are available at your local garden center. They are little clumps of creeping type grasses in trays. You plant them on 12 to 18 inch centers and stand by the lawnmower waiting for them to grow into a solid mass of rich green turf. Plugging is not cheap, but if you can only do a little of your yard at a time it is an excellent way to do it. It will take anywhere from a couple months to a year or more for the plugs to become united into a lawn. This will depend a lot on your ability to water frequently and fertilize on schedule. The garden center that wants to sell you the plugs will advise you on the best varieties for your area and supply you with complete planting instructions.

3.   SEEDING the lawn is for those with infinite patience. Bahia grasses, centipede, common Bermuda (not the best variety) and carpet grass can all be grown from seed.

First you will need to prepare the seedbed by annihilating all existing vegetation with a properly applied universal herbicide like Round-Up. After waiting the prescribed length of time (usually one to two weeks), rake and smooth the soil, then apply your favorite seed. A good garden center will have people there that can advise you on the type of grass seed to plant for your specific needs. Don't hesitate to consult the local agricultural extension office as well. They are the experts and can provide you with numerous updated information bulletins on turf grasses.

You can get a more even coverage if you sow the seed at half the recommended rate going north-south and then go over your lawn a second time walking from east to west. Yeah, we know it sounds like a lot of extra work covering the same area twice, but the resulting turf will be much more even.

If possible you can give a light top dressing (a thin layer of good quality top soil) to conserve soil moisture and hide the seed from hungry birds. If top dressing isn't a workable idea then rake heavily over the bed once the seed has been scattered. This will work most of the seed into the soil.

It is generally a good idea to water daily while you are waiting for the seeded lawn to turn green and begin to look like the neighbor's. You can apply a light application of granular slow-release fertilizer when you are preparing the seed bed or about the time the adolescent grass is ready for it's first mowing. Feeding after the grass is growing is more efficient, but remember that to be most effective fertilizer should be applied several hours after a good watering so that the plant's systems are most able to take advantage of the nutrients and there is less danger of burning.

WHAT TO DO WITH THE WEEDS, BUGS AND DISEASES IN YOUR FLORIDA LAWN

In the golden age of suburbia the ultimate goal of the lawn was CONTROL. The mere sight of an uninvited plant growing in your yard was viewed as a challenge. After all, isn't it you vs. nature? You even took your neighbor to court if he didn't spray gallons of poison on the fleabane or spurge growing against his fence. CONTROL wasn't limited to undesirable plant life either. It extended to small animals, insects (every insect), neighborhood pets and small children. We were once so concerned with control and uniformity that if the lawn didn't look like Astroturf, we raced to the garden center to buy whatever it took to control it. Even some of the valued grass you planted became the enemy if it grew too dark, too tall or in any other way did not conform.

Today, we are moving toward a sense of cooperation with nature instead of violent opposition. Once we attacked with aerosols, hose-end sprayers and bags of expensive poisons when we even thought we might see a bug, now we talk about acceptable population levels for such enemies as mole crickets and sod webworms.

Instead of recommending periodic applications of broad spectrum pesticides designed to kill the good, the bad and the ugly before finding its way into your water table, we are now beginning to use natural controls and the trend is growing rapidly. Here are just a few examples:

- Thuricide compounds that attack sod webworms, but do not harm bees, earthworms and other useful critters like earwigs and spiders.
- Developing populations of natural predators that feed on fire ants, chinch bugs, mole crickets etc. Remember ladybugs and the praying mantis?
- Puerto Rico has a parasitic wasp and a predatory nematode that keep their mole cricket populations under control. We have scientists researching their potential for Florida lawns.
- We will soon have on the market non-poisonous materials that will be sprayed on your lawn that make the grass so distasteful to the bugs that they move over to the neighbor's lawn.
- You will go to the garden center and buy a little vial of bug perfume (pheromones) that attract amorous moths to traps.

This is only the beginning of research on working with nature to produce a backyard that is more in harmony with the real world around us than in opposition to it. This will mean we may be able to relax a little bit and enjoy some of the plants growing here before the landscaping services started creating formal meticulously manicured estates. We are learning to lighten up and enjoy the life beyond the air conditioner and in order to do that we have to make our great outdoors safer for us to inhabit.

The average suburbanite spends ten times as much on pesticides for his lawn as the average farmer does for the crops that are his livelihood. These chemicals are valuable tools, but they can inflict harm in ways we don't yet understand on generations not yet born. We have to use these tools with caution and wisdom.

FIVE WAYS TO AVOID PROBLEMS IN YOUR LAWN

Prevention is a whole lot easier than curing these insect and disease problems.

1. A good healthy turf is the best deterrent to weeds, insects and disease. Healthy lawns start with planning and then planting the proper grass or ground cover for the soil type, water availability and sun-shade ratio. Healthy vigorously growing plants have a natural resistance to many of the above problems. Planting a sun-loving St. Augustine like Floratine under a centuries old oak is going to give you constant problems.
Every year brings new disease and insect resistant varieties. True, the newly patented ones cost more, but research and development isn't cheap. The increased expense for these improved varieties is nothing compared to what the resistance can save you in pesticides, effort and frustration.
2. You can feed your lawn too much or too often and this will produce spurts of tender growth and these obese, overfed plants are weak and unable to resist insects and disease. Using cheap fast release fertilizers can give your turf a feast and famine cycle that also produces weak plants. The easiest way to avoid this problem is to follow the recommended feeding schedule for the type of grass you planted.

3.   Improper use of insecticides and fungicides can burn, damage and even kill turf. Remember these are poisons designed to kill. Applying chemicals to a heat or drought stressed lawn can cause a lot more damage than the bugs you were after. Whatever you do don't apply a stronger mix than the container recommends. DO EXACTLY WHAT THE LABEL SAYS.

4.   Proper mowing is also important in preventing disease problems. Cut at a sufficient height to help conserve moisture and leave enough blade to produce food for the plant. When you scalp your lawn it isn't dense enough to crowd out the weeds. Using the proper type mower and a sharp mower blade can also prevent the kind of tearing damage that fungus spores love.

5.   Watering is also a key. Avoid watering too frequently. Don't water so that the turf is going to go into the nighttime hours wet. This can encourage disease too.

GRASS ISN'T THE ONLY ANSWER

The Florida climate, in cooperation with Mamma Nature and the Florida nursery industry, provides you with a wealth of alternatives to grass and as we move toward more natural landscaping we will see more of these labor saving, and water saving ground covers in use. In shady areas where grass is a constant challenge you also have the option of ferns, ivies, liriope, dwarf mondo, pygmy bamboo, confederate jasmine, Asiatic jasmine, cast iron plant, and in the Southern part of the state you can even use spathaphylum, begonias, bromeliads and a whole lot more.

With the increasing use of drought tolerant planting (Xeroscaping) there are options for those sunny dry areas as well. There are numerous creeping lantanas, society garlic, some junipers, Rhoeo discolor (Moses-in-the-bulrushes) and many more.

You don't have to limit your lawn just to grass. It's boring, labor intensive and in many ways unnatural. Enjoy some of the variety life has to offer. There is a wealth of ground cover material available in Florida. The following are just a few suggestions for specific situations. Note: the N, C and S simply mean this plant is recommended for north, central or south Florida.

LOW GROWING GROUND COVERS FOR SHADY AREAS

Asiatic jasmine	NCS	non-flowering vine
Coromandel	S	vine with white, pink or purple flowers most of the year
Dwarf azaleas	NC	various heights and colors
Dwarf mondo grass	NCS	6 to 10 inches; great substitute for grass
English ivy	NCS	vine; many varieties
Grape ivy	S	vigorous vine; several varieties
Holly fern	NCS	2 foot evergreen
Liriope	NCS	1 to 2 feet; purple or white flowers, evergreen foliage
Oyster plant (Rhoeo discolor)	CS	1 to 2 feet; purple foliage
Pygmy bamboo	NCS	4 to 8 inches; deep green or variegated
Setcreasea colors	NCS	12 to 15 inches; various foliage colors
Wandering Jew	NCS	6 to 10 inches; various foliage colors
Wedelia	NCS	12 to 15 inches; yellow flowers

TALL GROUND COVERS FOR MODERATELY SHADY AREAS

Asparagus fern	NCS	1 to 3 feet; white flowers and red berries
Azaleas	NC	variable height and color
Impatiens	NCS	1 to 3 feet; great color; will freeze
Leather leaf fern	NCS	3 feet; rugged evergreen
Mint	NCS	1 to 3 feet; color, fragrance and utility
Shrimp plant	NCS	3 to 6 feet easy
Wax begonia	NCS	1 to 2 feet; great color; will freeze

SALT TOLERANT GROUND COVERS

Dwarf junipers	NC	various heights; some varieties are somewhat salt tolerant
English ivy	NCS	somewhat tolerant
Holly fern	NCS	2 feet; somewhat tolerant
Hottentot fig	CS	6 inches; yellow or pink flowers; very salt tolerant
Leather leaf fern	NCS	3 feet; somewhat tolerant
Liriope	NCS	1 foot; somewhat tolerant
Oyster plant	CS	1 to 2 feet; somewhat tolerant
Wedelia	NCS	yellow flowers; very salt tolerant

FLOWERING GROUND COVERS FOR FULL SUN

African iris	NCS	3 to 4 feet; cream or white flowers
Creeping lantana	NCS	various colors; blooms most of year
Dwarf azaleas	NC	various colors; not all do well in full sun
Hottentot fig	CS	6 inches; yellow or pink flowers
Japanese honeysuckle	NCS	vine with fragrant white flowers
Mexican heather (cuphea hyssopifolia)	CS	1 to 2 feet; pink, purple or white flowers most of year
Society garlic	NCS	2 to 3 feet; lavender flowers much of the year
Strawberry	NC	6 inches; flowers and fruit
Wedelia	CS	yellow flowers much of the year

DROUGHT TOLERANT GROUND COVERS

Asparagus fern	NCS	1 to 3 feet
Creeping lantana	NCS	12 to 24 inches
English ivy	NCS	vine
Holly fern	NCS	2 feet; evergreen
Hottentot fig	CS	6 inches; yellow or pink flowers
Japanese honeysuckle	NCS	rugged vine
Leather leaf fern	NCS	3 feet; evergreen
Liriope	NCS	1 foot
Oyster plant	CS	1 to 2 feet; purple leaves
Setcreasea	NCS	12 to 15 inches; various foliage colors
Wedelia	NCS	12 to 18 inches; yellow flowers

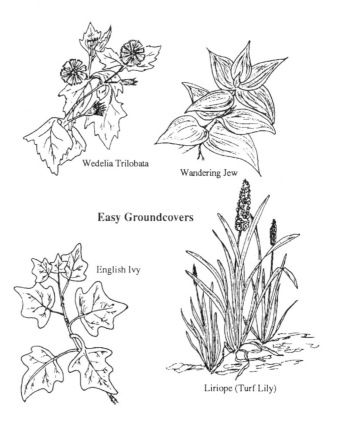

Wedelia Trilobata

Wandering Jew

Easy Groundcovers

English Ivy

Liriope (Turf Lily)

SECTION FOUR

FLORIDA SOILS ARE UNIQUE

If you have stepped off the sidewalk almost anywhere in our fair state you probably stepped into sand, or grass growing on top of sand. Florida is a statewide sand pile, except for those areas where limestone or muck bogs create a greater problem.

One of our more sarcastic friends suggested that we need to tax every tourist that comes into the state five pounds of topsoil. "No matter where they call home the soil there has got to be better than what we've got here," she claimed.

Good soil in Florida is any soil that will make plants grow. This isn't much different than anyplace else. Plants are adaptable and will grow in many variations of this blend of air, water, mineral material and organic matter we refer to as soil. Not all plants were designed by nature to grow in the same soil type and that's one of the good points a Florida gardener has with all this sand. True, sand isn't very good at holding water and nutrients leach out quickly, but it is easier to make sand into the kind of soil you need than clay, or shale or limestone. It's a lot easier to put a shovel into as well.

Most of us Yankees come down here from areas where good soil is taken for granted. Up there you and I mixed a little compost or peat moss into the hole when we planted a tree, gave it a good spring feeding then spent the summer mowing grass and sitting in the shade listening to the ball game. We come to a state where that's not enough. This doesn't mean we should all give up, buy a few silk flowers to brighten the flower beds, retreat to the couch and turn up the air conditioner.

Sand is a lot like flour. By adding different materials to flour you can produce bread, chocolate cake or toll house cookies. You add sugar, or yeast, or shortening, or any of a multitude of other items and get deliciously different results. You can make the sand into whatever type of soil you desire by adding organic matter, using fertilizers or altering the pH to suit the temperament of whatever it is you are trying to grow.

Sand also has another advantage in a state where the rainfall can exceed fifty inches a year. Sand has extremely good drainage, sometimes too good, because it doesn't hold moisture for when it's needed. For most plants a soil that is about 25 percent water is ideal. Another problem with sand is that when water is applied it goes straight down. There is no lateral spread because there is little organic matter to carry the moisture by osmosis from the end of the sprinkler's spray to the next plant. This is another reason for compost, cow manure or peat. It helps to hold some of the moisture and it will also help to spread moisture in the soil. This, in turn, will encourage more aggressive root systems.

Probably the best single item you can add to your sand to make it into soil is also the cheapest. Build a compost pile and recycle every waste product you produce that's organic. The carcasses of weeds encountered in the flower beds can thus become food for the next crop of petunias. Spent bean stalks and corn husks will feed the next generation of carrots, lettuce and squash. What you trimmed from the azaleas this year will, next year, provide a healthy soil for the sago palm or rose bush you can't resist buying.

Composting sounds like a lot of work to those who haven't done it, but it's easier than stuffing all the trimmings, peelings, dinner scraps, clippings, fallen leaves, etc. into plastic bags and paying to have them hauled away. Compost does not smell, does not need to be unsightly and does not attract bugs or harbor disease. You can get great detailed information on composting from the local Agricultural Extension office.

SOIL ADDITIVES

All soils are alive! Dirt from the backyard is teeming with microscopic critters busily munching on minerals, breaking down leaves, twigs and used roots into the building blocks of another tree, blade of grass or dollar weed. Even the poorest excuse for soil contains millions of bacteria, fungi, insects and more. The better the soil, the more organic matter you have worked into it, the bigger the population it can support. This makes a more hospitable home for the roots of your chosen plants.

There are many organic materials that can be added to your sandy soil to generally improve quality or help solve special problems.

1. BLOOD MEAL is a slaughterhouse by-product. It is a natural source of nitrogen and some claim it will discourage rabbits, but it doesn't bother squirrels at all.

2. COTTONSEED MEAL is also a great source of nitrogen.

3. BONE MEAL is another slaughterhouse by-product. This one provides lots of phosphorous for bulbs and root crops.

4. MILORGANITE is a product of the Milwaukee Sewage Commission and is exactly what you think. Treated sewage sludge is a great natural fertilizer, soil conditioner and amendment. It is used extensively on golf courses. Many local municipal sewage treatment plants will give the stuff away. All you need to do is bring your own container.

5. MUSHROOM MANURE is the used growing medium from mushroom farming. Again this is a very inexpensive organic additive to your lawn and garden. You can get it by the truck load if you live near a mushroom farm.

6. COMPOSTED COW MANURE is a feedlot by-product that has been aged. Usually it is mixed with peat humus and may have little nutrient value, but is still a good soil conditioner. It is completely safe to use and is odorless.

7. DEHYDRATED COW MANURE is a dried version of the above product with several key differences. The nutrient value is higher, thus improperly applied it can cause some burning. It isn't 60 percent water so you are getting more for your money. More of the dehydrated manures are pure rather than being cut with peat humus, but this isn't an odor free product.

8. RABBIT, CHICKEN, HORSE AND OTHER ANIMAL MANURES are also valuable and often locally available at little cost. They are best used after they have aged. Fresh manures can cause serious burn on your plants.

9. SPHAGNUM PEAT is sometimes referred to as Canadian or milled peat. It's great at retaining soil moisture and promoting root growth. Generally, sphagnum peat is weed seed free and retards some fungus. Since it is usually sold in compressed bales by volume rather than weight you get a bigger value for your investment. Suggestion to make it easier to work with this material: cut a hole in the bag and soak it well with the hose the day before you are going to apply it.

10. PEAT HUMUS is also known as muck or black peat. Up north it was that old friend we called Michigan peat. This is raised on muck farms and often contains weed seed. The pH can vary dramatically, but because it is cheap it is used extensively and even though it deteriorates quickly in the soil, it does serve as a good soil conditioner. Since it is sold by weight you are buying a fair amount of water in each bag, but it is still inexpensive.

11. COMMUNITY COMPOST is something new on the scene. To avoid landfill mountains of prunings, grass clippings and other lawn waste many communities are now collecting, chipping or shredding and composting these items. This in turn is sold by the pickup load or in some areas by the bag. Commercial landscapers are using this, but the consumer hasn't caught on yet.

IT'S ALL A MATTER OF CHEMISTRY

The above listed soil amendments are primarily to make the sand more suitable as a home for your trees, shrubs, flowers and vegetables. When you add any of these organic soil conditioners to the site before planting you are increasing moisture retention, encouraging the growth of soil organisms that help breakdown nutrients into chemical compounds the plants can use, preventing fertilizers from leaching out of the soil as quickly and providing some nutrient value.

Remember, soil conditioners are not fertilizers however. In this sandy soil you may still need to use some additional plant foods to achieve the same results they do at the theme parks. We don't want to bore you with a thesis on soil science, but there is a little bit of basic chemistry you should know. Here's a little bit of homework for you. Go out to the garage, or wherever you store bags, bottles and boxes of plant foods and read the label. It will tell you the contents, much like the bag of corn chips or breakfast cereal does. And the numbers are just as confusing. Hold onto that label. We will come back to it in a few minutes, but first we are going to talk about the numbers and break the cryptic code.

The big numbers, like 12-4-8 or 6-6-6 tell you the percentage of the three primary nutrients. If a fertilizer contains the following three macro-nutrients it is called COMPLETE.

1.   NITROGEN (N) is the first element listed in the code. It can be in two forms: Fast release (inorganic or soluble) nitrogen which gives you quick green up, but it's like empty calories. Your plants are hungry again in a matter of weeks. This fast release nitrogen can burn the leaves of the very plants it was supposed to be feeding if applied too heavily, to plants stressed by lack of water or when the temperature is too high.

Slow release (organic or insoluble) nitrogen takes longer to breakdown into forms the plants can use, thus it continues to feed over a long period of time. In Florida's sandy soil some of the slow release nitrogen may leach away before your plants get to use it.

Nitrogen is important for leaf growth and general vigor in your plants. A lack of sufficient nitrogen will result in stunted growth and a general pale appearance, but too much will cause weak rampant growth and failure to flower.

2.   The second number is PHOSPHOROUS or PHOSPHATE (P) and it's necessary for flowering and fruiting. It increases disease resistance, encourages root development, food storage capability and hastens maturity. A lack of phosphorous will result in poor bloom and sometimes browning on the edges of mature leaves. Too much phosphorous can result in a reddish or purple tint to leaves and stems and irregular growth. You can purchase bone meal or super-phosphate if you need to provide more of this nutrient than a balanced fertilizer contains.

3.   POTASSIUM or POTASH (K) is the third of the big three nutrients and it's vital for photosynthesis and the plant's ability to handle adverse weather and disease. A shortage of potassium will cause a general lack of vigor, yellow or brownish leaf tips and margins, weak stems and poor seed production. If you need an extra jolt of potassium you can get muriate of potash at most garden centers, but apply it with caution and follow directions.

Beyond the big three chemicals in the fertilizer bag are usually some of the following minor elements, sometimes referred to as micro-nutrients.

1.   MAGNESIUM which is vital for new growth and is usually deficient in Florida soils. Curling and frizzle-leaf fronds on palms are often the result of a need for magnesium. It can be applied as dolomitic limestone or magnesium sulphate (epsom salts).

2.   MANGANESE is involved in plant growth and in the production of seeds, but it's also needed to keep the soil organisms healthy that break down unusable materials into the necessary elements.

3.   IRON is necessary in the formation of chlorophyll and yellow leaves with green veins indicate a lack of iron. Without iron the plant can't use other nutrients, even when they are present.

4.   BORON is needed for flower formation. A lack of boron can result in bud drop or deformed flowers, small or deformed leaves and sometimes corky growths on leaf and stem.

5.   COPPER (Cu) is another aid in disease resistance and a tendency toward mildew or fungus problems can be the result of a lack of copper.

6.   ZINC (Zn) is used in cell division and is vital in regulating plant growth. A lack of zinc can cause stunted growth, small thin leaves and a decrease in flowering.

7.   MOLYBDENUM (Mo) enables the plant to use nitrogen.

These trace minerals are all important for healthy growth and strong bodies for your lawn and garden. Most are in short supply in our typical Florida soil, but a good fertilizer will have most of what you need. You can purchase minor element mixtures in liquid and granular form, but be careful not to use too much because sometimes an overdose of the cure is worse than the deficiency.

Now go back to that label again. Look carefully and you will find instructions on how and when to apply this plant food and what plants it is recommended for and what ones will not respond well to it. Again we give the warning no one heeds, BEFORE YOU APPLY, READ THE DIRECTIONS, AND DON'T USE MORE THAN RECOMMENDED.

The big three are vital and the minor elements are all necessary, but there are a couple more nutrients we can't forget about. These elements aren't usually listed on the label of your fertilizer because their primary purpose is to correct the acidity level (pH) of the soil.

1.   SULPHUR (Sulfur) (S) is a soil acidifier that's necessary for the formation of plant proteins, but it does more than that. It serves as a fungicide, miticide and insecticide. Sulphur can be used to correct an alkaline, or sweet, soil or make a neutral soil acid enough for such plants as azaleas, gardenias, camellias and blueberries. It's wise to check the pH of your soil before adding sulphur. Aluminum sulfate is one commonly available form of this acidifier.

2.   CALCIUM (Ca) is vital for the formation of strong cell walls, general plant strength, disease and insect resistance. Without calcium growth may be stunted and weak. Calcium is used to neutralize a soil that is too acid. It's usually applied as garden lime, hydrated lime and dolomitic lime. Garden gypsum is a calcium sulfate that's often used to loosen clay soils.

A FEW THOUGHTS ON FERTILIZERS IN FLORIDA

If you were to watch the experts you would see them throw some peat moss or compost and a few shovels full of cheap fertilizer onto the soil, mix it in to a depth appropriate for what they're planting and start burying roots. We aren't saying you don't need to know all the chemistry above, it makes great after-dinner conversation, if you don't get fanatical about it. Florida sand can be made habitable by adding the organic matter and a fertilizer mix recommended for the plants you are going to set out.

Be careful not to apply fertilizers to plants that are stressed or dry. Water six to twelve hours before applying the nutrients. The plant's system is then ready for dinner and there is less chance of damage. A fertilizer uses moisture and if it draws it away from the leaves it can cause a dehydration called fertilizer burn.

The weather gets really hot down here (you may have noticed this) and it can cause damage if you fertilize lawns, flower beds and some vegetables in the heat of the day. Not to mention the stress it causes you.

Because the sandy excuse for a soil does such a poor job of holding onto nutrients it is necessary to fertilize more frequently down here than you had to up north.

The growing season is longer in Florida and you will find that it's necessary to feed flower beds and vegetable gardens all year long. Trees and shrubs will beg for extra meals and lawns will expect snacks.

MULCHES

A mulch is anything placed on the soil surface around a planting. It can be anything from bark chips to crushed marble or gravel. We have seen sawdust, shredded tabloids, pine needles and almost anything else imaginable used. A mulch serves several purposes including:

- Conserving soil moisture
- Keeping the soil temperature more even
- Helps to keep soil from washing when it rains
- As organic mulches decay they add nutrients to the soil
- Helps control the growth of weeds
- Looks better than sand

A DESERT IN A STATE SURROUNDED BY WATER

Almost all of Florida was at one time or another beachfront property. Our adopted state is geologically very young and in some ways is still developing. The problem is that sand doesn't hold water well. When it rains it gets wet, but in a day or two the sand pile has dried out and the plants are wilting. You can cope with this in a number of ways.

1. Praying for rain, rain dances and shooting cannonballs into the sky have all been tried with only modest success. By the way, depending on local ordinances, the cannon can get you into a lot of trouble and maybe even onto the evening news.

2. Mulches help to conserve some of the moisture.

3. A garden hose and a lot of patience can solve the problem.

4. In-ground irrigation is a durable and easy, but expensive way to keep your landscape green instead of brown.

5. A drip irrigation system is a good option for trees, flower beds and even some garden plants. It is easy to install and uses water efficiently.

6. You can plant rugged natives and relax.

NEMATODES, THE FLORIDA GARDENER'S BEST EXCUSE

Nematodes are for the most part too small to see with the naked eye or even bifocals, but they are out there. They are everywhere. They can be found in Ottawa, Detroit, Manhattan, even New Jersey; it's just that they are worse down here. Every handful of soil you pick up will have hundreds or thousands of these little worm-like critters in it. Most are not of the harmful sort and they do serve a purpose in soil health and natural balance. Few native plants are seriously bothered by them, but the problem is you want to grow things like roses, figs, gardenias and some grasses that don't belong here.

Not all nematodes prey on the roots of plants, but the ones that do – the most common is referred to as root knot nematode – generally cause swollen, ugly gnarled growths on the roots that interfere with water and nutrient absorption. They don't kill a plant overnight, but cause a gradual decline over a season or even several years. You blame yourself and feed and water more, or you blame the weather, the neighbors or the current occupant of the White House, but the problem is underground and can't be seen unless you dig up the roots.

These micro-beasts are most active in the top twelve to fifteen inches of the soil. Some gardeners try to outsmart the critters by cutting the bottom out of a big black nursery pot and planting their pet rose or whatever in good topsoil inside the pot. When the roots grow out of the pot they are below the major nematode zone. It may sound like a lot of work, but it can be successful.

It has also been suggested by many garden experts that the greater the organic content of the soil the more natural controls there are on the nematode population. This is another good reason to keep working the compost and manures into the soil.

There are also organic materials that seem to limit nematode damage when worked into the soil surface around existing plantings, but the most effective way to control them is to sterilize the soil. There are basically two ways this can be achieved. Dangerous chemicals like Vapam can be used (there are also several other restricted chemicals that require a professional license to apply).

The safest and cheapest way to reduce their numbers though is a simple process called solarization.

- Till the area to be treated to smooth the surface if needed.

- Soak the area thoroughly. The soil needs to be wet for this to be effective.

- Cover with clear plastic, not black. Under clear plastic the soil temperature will rise to 120 degrees or more and this is enough to do in most of the critters.

- Make certain the edges of the plastic are buried or covered with soil so that the heat doesn't escape.

- Sit back and wait for four to six weeks.

- Remove the plastic and till in some good rich compost.

- Plant to your little heart's content.

There have been claims that several plants like sweet potato, marigold and garlic discourage nematodes. Scientific studies haven't been conclusive yet, but it certainly isn't going to hurt to have some marigolds brightening the vegetable garden or garlic providing some accent to the rose bed.

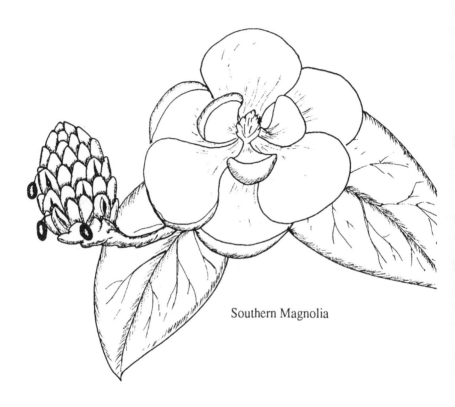

Southern Magnolia

SECTION FIVE

THE FLORIDA LANDSCAPE

TREES: TRADITIONAL AND TROPICAL

We move to Florida and we are enchanted with swaying palms, exotic fruits, tropical trees that bloom in the winter and all the other charms of Margaritaville. But, sooner or later, IT HAPPENS. You wake up some spring morning and miss the Japanese weeping cherry that you had planted so lovingly by the sidewalk you left behind. You long for the brilliance of fall foliage. Your mind begins to catalog each year's additions to the backyard you left behind. You rush out to the garden center and learn the awful truth. There is a deep dark secret the real estate people don't tell you about Florida. If they had been honest about it you might not have moved down here. They didn't tell you blue spruce doesn't grow in Florida.

It is so easy to accept orange trees outside the door, sandhill cranes strolling across the backyard and even the ever-present lizards that are a part of the Florida lifestyle. What we can't accept is what isn't a part of living in the subtropics.

"Why?" you shout at the garden center clerk, "don't you carry spruce and cherries? I want a red delicious apple, and while you're at it can't you order me about a dozen lilac bushes?"

The poor clerk only shakes his head.

These are all plants that enjoy a good winter. We have a theory that it's because trees don't have to shovel snow. Why else would they refuse to adapt to perpetual summer? The fact is there are several reasons why they won't survive down here, no matter how hard you try.

- Many trees, shrubs and other plants that live "up there" need the cold winter weather to regulate their growth cycle.

- The fruit and flowering trees you were familiar with may require a certain number of chill hours (hours when the temperature is below forty degrees Fahrenheit) to set the buds for next year's blossoms.

81

- They can't cope with Florida's soils or the organisms found in that soil.

- The humidity encourages fungus and disease problems they don't have a natural resistance to.

- The insects never stop dining, or multiplying either, in Florida. There are bugs that the northern plants and trees have never met before and have no experience defending themselves against.

There a few old friends from the north that do seem to thrive in this state, or at least the north and central parts of it. These are for the most part natives that are available in most good garden centers. Not only do they bring you a touch of home, they can take all the abuse Florida can throw at them.

American holly (many native and improved Florida varieties)
Arborvitae (an old evergreen favorite that adapts well)
Flowering dogwood (the basic white variety does well; pink and double forms are poor performers)
Fringe tree (a great flowering native that is underplanted even in the north)
Mimosa (pink flowers, lacy leaves, spreading crown. What more do you want?)
Redbud (the ideal companion to the dogwood)
River birch (not paper white, but peeling tan bark is as close as we can get)
Sycamore (a magnificent large tree anywhere)
Tulip tree (should be planted more in Florida where a large tree is suitable)

SHADE AND FLOWERING TREES IN THE LANDSCAPE

Only a few years ago it was common practice to clear a lot of every tree, shrub, sprig and weed before the developer did anything else. All existing vegetation was stripped away to create a barren mini-desert. Now we're somewhat wiser. We try to save as many trees as possible. Sometimes the roots are damaged so severely that the trees only survive a few years before turning into firewood, but at least it's wise to make the effort.

There are many reasons to keep trees in the landscape, and their value goes far beyond aesthetics.

- Shade, in a state where the sun shines almost all the time, is more than just a good idea; it is a necessity.

- Your air conditioning bill can be reduced by 20 percent or more with a few well placed trees. This is a benefit you can put in the bank. The life of your roofing shingles can be extended also.

- The property value is increased. Without trees your house looks like little more than a box sitting in a sand pile.

- Take a deep breath. You do this all day long, your life depends on the oxygen you inhale. Isn't it convenient that one full grown oak tree puts enough oxygen in the air each day to keep you breathing for twenty-four hours?

- Taking care of the fallen leaves is a great source of exercise. Raking uses muscles you didn't know you had.

- Trees attract wildlife. Birds and squirrels nest in the trees and consume millions of bugs, weed seeds and ripening strawberries.

- Trees help remove pollution from the air. They help to clean up the garbage we put into the atmosphere we expect our children and grandchildren to breathe.

- Trees can also provide some privacy and help control noise pollution.

- Many of the trees you can plant in your home landscape also provide flowers and fruit. There is nothing wrong with what is sometimes referred to as a "working landscape".

- Trees also play a role in controlling soil erosion. Their roots hold soil against the onslaught of Florida's storms.

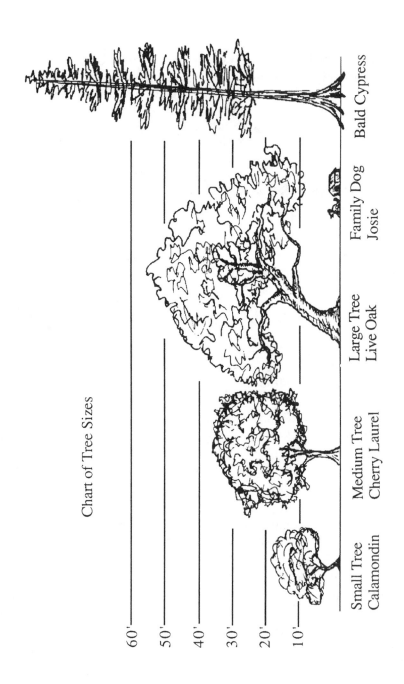

Chart of Tree Sizes

Small Tree
Calamondin

Medium Tree
Cherry Laurel

Large Tree
Live Oak

Family Dog
Josie

Bald Cypress

60'
50'
40'
30'
20'
10'

SELECTING THE RIGHT TREE FOR YOUR FLORIDA LANDSCAPE

Many texts divide trees into either shade or flowering, but we have always questioned this way of categorizing them. Almost all flowering trees are also good at casting shade. It is more helpful to list trees by their mature size so that you can plan ahead rather than by what the flower looks like. For that reason the following lists include a combination of trees that cast both shade and flowers, sometimes even fruit and are listed as small trees (under 30 feet), medium trees (30 to 50 feet) or large trees (over 50 feet).

SMALL TREES FOR THE LANDSCAPE: These trees are ideal for the smaller lot, as an accent in the foreground of larger specimens, as a screen or in the softening of harsh architectural lines. The following is a brief list of some of the easier small trees that are commonly available. We have also noted which sections of Florida they are suited to: N (North), C (Central) and S (South).

Tree	Region	Description
Bottlebrush (Callistemon)	NCS	Red flowers throughout spring
Brazilian pepper (Schinus terebinthifolius)	CS	Red berries on female at Christmas
Chaste tree (Vitex agnus-castus)	NCS	Spikes of white or lavender flowers all summer; salt tolerant
Crape myrtle (Lagerstroemia indica)	NCS	Florida's answer to the lilac; sorry, no fragrance
Dogwood, flowering (Cornus florida)	NC	A native you know from up north
Jerusalem thorn (Parkinsonia aculeata)	NCS	Fragrant yellow flowers in spring and summer; has thorns
Loquat (Eriobotrya japonica)	NCS	Spicy flowers in fall; tasty fruit in late winter
Orchid tree (Bauhinia)	CS	Purple, red or white flowers
Pomegranate (Punica granatum)	NCS	Striking scarlet flowers and unique flavorful fruit
Redbud (Cercis canadensis)	NC	Pink flowers in early spring; versatile in landscape
Screw pine (Pandanus utilis)	S	Dramatic novelty growth habit
Southern red cedar (Juniperus silicicola)	NCS	Attractive evergreen, should be used more; salt tolerant
Wax myrtle (Myrica cerifera)	NCS	Southern cousin of the bayberry; excellent small tree

MEDIUM SIZE TREES FOR THE LANDSCAPE: These trees are the ideal height and spread for the medium size lot, cast plentiful shade and help bring large specimens into balance. You will need to keep in mind that these trees grow to a height of thirty to fifty feet and may develop a crown broader than that. The average home grounds can accommodate only a couple of these so select carefully. Again this is not a complete list, but only some suggestions that are easy to grow and can be found without the search becoming a quest.

American holly (Ilex opaca, var.)	NC	Many varieties of this old friend, East Palatka one of most common
Black olive (Bucida buceras)	S	Superior shade tree; salt tolerant
Bradford pear	NC	Another old friend from the north; white flowers
Camellia (Camellia japonica)	NC	Magnificent bloom in winter
Camphor tree (Cinnamomum camphora)	NCS	Almost a large tree; aromatic foliage; evergreen
Cherry laurel (Prunus caroliniana)	NC	Fragrant white flowers; can be trained as tree or shrub
Chinese elm (Ulmus parvifolia)	NC	Several varieties, some are evergreen; mottled bark
Chinaberry (Melia azedarach)	NCS	Fragrant lavender-blue flowers in spring; fast growing; weak wood
Golden raintree (Koelreuteria formosana)	NC	Yellow flowers followed by pink seed husks
Jacaranda (Jacaranda acutifolia)	CS	Lavender-blue flowers in large clusters in May and June
Loblolly bay (Gordonia lasianthus)	NCS	White flowers in spring and summer; upright growth
Lychee (Litchi chinensis)	CS	Bright red clusters of fruit on an attractive tree
Sea hibiscus (Hibiscus tileaceus)	CS	Flowers are yellow in morning, maroon by evening
Weeping willow (Salix babylonica)	NC	Another old friend from the north

LARGE TREES FOR THE LANDSCAPE: Large trees used carelessly in the landscape can result in overcrowding, a house lost in the jungle and shade so dense little else can be grown in the landscape. Remember that these trees do grow up, plan ahead and plant with caution. The following are only some of the massive Florida trees you might want to consider.

Bombax (Bombax malabaricum)	S	Bright red flowers in winter followed by seed pods filled with silk
Floss silk tree (Chorisa speciosa)	S	Pink flowers in fall; blunt thorns on trunk; seed pod filled with cotton floss
Gumbo-limbo (Bursea simaruba)	S	Rapid growing native tree, a classic where there is room
Laurel oak (Quercus laurifolia)	NCS	Short lived; upright growth
Live oak (Quercus virginiana)	NCS	Florida's best shade tree; long lived; wide canopy
Magnolia, southern (Magnolia grandiflora)	NC	Symbol of the South; large white fragrant flowers in late spring
Norfolk Island pine (Araucaria excelsa)	CS	You remember this as a house plant; striking in your landscape
Red maple (Acer rubrum)	NC	Another old friend from the North
River birch (Betula nigra)	NC	Excellent, almost medium size tree; effective near water
Silk oak (Grevillea robusta)	CS	Orange flowers in spring; rapid growing, massive tree
Sweet gum (Liquidambar styraciflua)	NCS	An old northern friend; fast growing dark red fall foliage
Tulip tree (Liriodendron tulipifera)	NC	Far too large for most home grounds; greenish-yellow flowers in spring

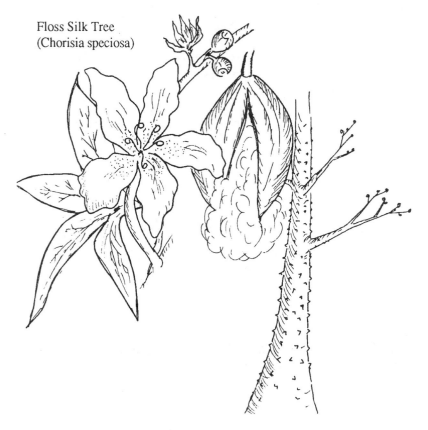

Floss Silk Tree
(Chorisia speciosa)

Big pink flowers in autumn, seed capsule filled with cotton floss

TRADITIONAL FRUIT TREES may also have a place in your Florida landscape. Varieties of apples, peaches, pears, plums, apricots and nectarines all grow and bear fruit here. Most of these are limited to the north and central parts of the state where there are sufficient chill hours.

PLANTING TREES IN YOUR LANDSCAPE

The most common error we make when selecting and planting trees is our failure to consider mature size. Trees planted a few feet apart may look almost lonely when they are only a few feet tall, but it's a jungle when they reach thirty or fifty feet in height. They are overcrowded and ripe for health problems, not to mention the fact that you might have trouble finding your way up an overgrown driveway. Plan ahead for growth and allow sufficient space. After you've controlled this natural urge to overplant, it's time to get to work.

1. Dig a hole at least a foot deeper and wider than the container or root mass of the new addition to the backyard community. A larger hole will be better. The soil from this hole can be piled on a sheet of plastic or a tarp to avoid damage to the grass if you so desire. Mix some compost or other organic matter with it (about a third compost to two thirds soil is a good mix).

2. If you want to mix some fertilizer in the soil mix be careful not to overdo it. This can cause root burn and actually delay growth. It is better to wait until there is some new growth before feeding with anything other than a starter solution.

3. Put some of your prepared soil back in the hole so that the root mass will sit slightly higher than it did in the container. This is because the soil will settle a little.

4. Add some soil and soak well with the hose. Add more soil and soak again. This helps to avoid air pockets and barriers between soil and root mass.

5. Make certain the tree is straight and tamp soil well. It may be necessary to stake if the tree is large. We recommend using two or three stakes with wire run through a piece of old hose. A small tree usually doesn't need to be staked.

6. You can build a collar of soil four to six inches high around the tree in a two or three foot circle. This can serve as a watering well to prevent runoff when you water. You can also use a drip irrigation system very effectively on newly transplanted landscape trees.

7. If you feel you must give the new tree something to eat you can use a weak starter solution, but it isn't really necessary.

8. Prune back any long branches, damaged twigs and sucker shoots growing on the trunk. If you are planting a grafted tree remove any shoots growing from below the graft union.

9. Water deeply two or three times a week until the tree is established.

10. Once new growth starts you can begin a feeding program. Follow the directions on the container.

SALT TOLERANT SHADE TREES

One of the problems many of us Yankees encounter when we get down here is adjusting to salt in the soil and even the water supply. We expect it with beachfront property, but we find salty water several miles inland and salt spray carries a lot farther than expected. The following is a short list of the many trees that are either very tolerant or at least somewhat salt tolerant to help you in selecting the trees for your coastal property. Avoid the temptation to buy the cheapest nursery stock available from a retailer that knows little about the product being sold. Don't hesitate to contact your local agricultural extension office or visit the local library.

VERY SALT TOLERANT SALT	SOMEWHAT TOLERANT
Southern red cedar	Norfolk Island pine
Australian pine	Podocarpus
Cajeput-tree	Wax myrtle
Sea hibiscus	Live oak
Tabebuia (some varieties)	Southern magnolia
Geiger tree	Loquat
	Yaupon holly
	Jerusalem thorn
	Brazilian pepper tree

DO YOU MISS THE FALL FOLIAGE?

If you miss the spectacular colors of fall that can be found almost everywhere else but here, there are a few trees you can plant to help spread some much needed color in our adopted state. The problem is that fall happens all at once in the north. Here fall color begins somewhere in October and continues through January.

Sweet gum ------------------------- Deep red or purple fall foliage
Dogwood --------------------------- Red berries and leaves
Redbud ----------------------------- Burgundy and brown foliage
Chinese tallow tree ----------------- Orange and purple fall leaves
Red maple -------------------------- Same as up there
Silver maple ----------------------- Yellow and brown leaves
Tulip tree -------------------------- Yellow and brown leaves
Drake or Chinese elm -------------- Yellow and tan foliage
River birch ------------------------- Yellow or brown foliage
Pin oak---------------------------- Red, bronze and brown foliage

Leaves for fall color (river birch, red maple, elm, sweet gum & pin oak)

Other trees with fall color (Oct. through Jan.) include flowering dogwoods, Chinese tallow tree, sycamore and redbud.

91

FLOWERING SHRUBS

Lush green foliage is nice, but let's face it, a landscape all in green can be boring. We came down here because winter up there was a black and white photo and we wanted some Kodachrome. After all, they call this state Florida, not Folia. We demand flowers and we want them all year long. It doesn't matter whether you settled in the Panhandle or the Keys, you expect color.

Know what? It's not that difficult. In fact, it's too easy. Finding flowering shrubs is no problem. The problem is knowing when to stop bringing them home. Too many of us displaced Yankees in a few short years end up with overcrowded backyards filled with an unorganized collection of "one-of-a-kinds."

Don't get us wrong. We aren't saying you should have a detailed landscaping master plan and never, ever, deviate from it. Part of the fun of gardening in Florida is the opportunity to discover something new in every garden center or nursery we visit. It's okay to experiment and try new unfamiliar plants, but first, before we buy, we need to find out all we can about the little charmer that has made such an impression on us. If it isn't suitable or has special needs we can't meet, we should invest in something more compatible.

Also, exercise some restraint unless you are prepared to seize part of your neighbor's yard to house these additions to your botanical menagerie.

In the northern and central parts of Florida you have two great opportunities. If you are a winter resident you get to enjoy both to the fullest. If you are a full time resident here you have a great opportunity to harass friends and relatives stuck in the snow in Michigan, or Indiana or other points in the snow belt. You can send pictures of your camellias in bloom timed to the heaviest blasts of arctic weather where they live.

You know all about azaleas because you grew them up north, but the rules are slightly different here. First, they bloom in the winter months of January, February and March here and may throw some bloom at other odd times of the year. A variety called Red Ruffle is almost ever-blooming.

Camellias may be new to you, but you will grow to love them too. They are easy to care for, are reliable bloomers and require little in the way of special technique. The hibiscus is the last of the "big three" and is the most symbolic of the Florida we dreamed of when driving through slush and snow.

CAMELLIAS

These evergreen members of the tea family were brought here from the Orient in the late 1700s. Thomas Jefferson was one of the first to grow them and a few years later they were brought into Florida. Today there are literally thousands of varieties and plant societies limited solely to the cultivation of camellias. They are worthy of your consideration.

Camellias are comfortable as the background of your landscape, as a screen or tall hedge, or as a focal point. The deep glossy green leaves are striking, even when they aren't in bloom.

They prefer partial shade and insist on well-drained soil, but other than that they are not fussy. One word of caution though, they don't bloom heavily in dense shade and may get spindly.

Selecting the right camellia is not an easy task because there are single and double forms, semi-doubles, anemone or peony flowered and even rose flowered.

We recommend that you purchase plants when they are in bloom. This way you can see exactly what color and floral form you are getting as well as their blooming period. There are varieties of camellias that start blooming in September and others that are blooming as late as early April. By carefully selecting a few varieties you can have camellias in bloom almost half the year.

PLANTING CAMELLIAS

You can find camellias in bloom at the garden center in everything from one gallon pots to specimens twelve or fifteen feet tall. Buy the size that is easiest for you to handle. Don't worry, they will grow. In Florida they grow quickly.

They are tolerant of our sandy soils, but will perform much better if you work generous amounts of compost or other organic matter into the soil before planting. This should be as deep as you can go with eighteen to twenty-four inches almost ideal. At least three feet in diameter is also good. If you are planting a bed or hedge of camellias a roto-tiller is invaluable.

Remember that light shade is best. Too much sun and the leaves may scald; shade that's too dense and the growth is weak and bloom is scant.

They like a slightly acid soil (they will accept a pH between 5.0 and 6.5 without complaining). When you are preparing the soil you can mix some camellia food into the soil.

When planting disturb the roots as little as possible and water deeply, packing the soil around the root mass to eliminate air pockets. As is usually recommended, plant at the same depth the plants were growing in the containers.

You can apply a good mulch of pine needles, oak leaves or bark chips as the last step in giving your new camellia a good home. The mulch helps to keep the soil moist and cool while it controls the weeds.

After planting it is a good idea to water deeply two or three times a week until well established. After that you should only need to water during prolonged dry spells. Frequent watering can encourage healthy growth and heavier bloom. While different experts follow different schedules, one that seems to work for us is a feeding in February, late April, mid-July and November.

Camellias require little pruning, but damaged wood, errant branches or any growth you don't want should be trimmed off at your convenience. Pruning to shape or major surgery should be done in early spring, after flowering is over and new buds haven't been set yet.

AZALEAS

You are in Florida now so you can forget about the Exbury hybrids and the massive rhododendron, but this state gives you something with azaleas you couldn't get up there. Azaleas bloom in the winter down here. When they're planted in mass or as a border the effect can be breathtaking. That's why some cities and towns in Florida have annual azalea festivals.

Azaleas in Florida come in a variety of sizes and colors from the dwarf that never grows beyond two feet to formosas that can exceed eight feet in height. While azaleas are at their best in partial shade, there are varieties that can bask in the Florida sun without a whimper. Ask your local garden center or nursery what will be the best varieties for your needs.

PLANTING AZALEAS

Azaleas are acid loving plants and do well with a pH between 4.5 and 5.5. Like the camellias mentioned above, azaleas thrive when you work lots of compost or other organic matter (about 50-50 with your existing soil) into the planting site. This should be to a depth of twelve to eighteen inches for best results.

1.   Always water the plants and the site an hour or two before you are going to plant them. This helps to avoid stress and prevents the formation of a barrier between the root mass and the soil.

2.   Azaleas have a fibrous root mass that often needs stimulated to expand into the soil of its new home. You can do what the pros do and impress the neighbors. First remove the plant from the container. Then, with a sharp knife make three or four vertical cuts about 1/4 inch deep. This slight wounding encourages the formation of new roots and they, being young and adventurous, will explore the surrounding soil.

3.   Plant at the same depth the azalea was growing. These plants have a surface feeder root system and will literally suffocate if they are planted too deeply.

4.   After planting water well and press soil to eliminate air pockets.

5.   A good surface mulch of pine needles, oak leaves or bark chips is a must if you want your new azaleas to be happy. This protects the surface root system we mentioned earlier from drying out, coping with extremes of temperature and battling weeds.

6.   Azaleas are rugged and willingly handle a lot of abuse and neglect, but they must have water, especially the first year. Water deeply two or three times a week.

After azaleas are established they respond well to a regular feeding with azalea fertilizer. We don't recommend feeding while they are in bloom or when they have been drought stressed. Established and well mulched azaleas should need watered only during prolonged dry spells, unless they are growing in full sun.

Azaleas can, and should be, pruned. Don't be afraid to trim them back to the size or shape you want. They can even be sheared into a formal hedge, if that suits your landscape. We will suggest that you do this trimming shortly after blooming or at least before the end of July so that you don't remove a large portion of the next season's flowers.

HIBISCUS

The big three of Florida flowering shrubs are the camellia, azalea and hibiscus. While the first two are happiest in the northern and central parts of the state, the hibiscus longs for its native tropics and basks in the sun and warmth of south Florida, accepts central Florida, but struggles with the cold the farther north it goes.

Hundreds of named varieties grace the garden centers. All shades of yellow, orange, pink, red, white and even a few combinations are available in single and double forms. For those of us accustomed to shoveling snow, a shrub full of six or eight inch bright colored blossoms in the middle of winter is more than we can handle. The hibiscus has been called the queen of Florida flowers and Florida's best landscape plant by many professionals. Look at what this shrub has to offer the gardener from central Florida south.

1.   It is virtually everblooming. Even when a frost prunes the plant back to the soil line it quickly returns with enthusiasm.

2.   It is easy. In fact, once established it is almost care free, needing only occasional pruning to keep it in check.

3.   It's evergreen and the bright foliage provides an effective contrast to the flowers and provides an effective screen.

4.   It is versatile in the landscape. You can trim it into a hedge, use it as a foundation plant, accent or focal point.

5.   It will grow quite well in full sun or light shade and accepts almost any well drained soil, although hibiscus, like most landscape material, is happier in an organic soil.

You will often see offered for sale in your favorite garden center dwarfed hibiscus. These are not plants that are going to stay one or two feet tall forever. They aren't a dwarf variety; they have been treated with a growth retardant that will keep them compact for several months. Ultimately, they will begin to assume their normal growth habit and then it is up to you to prune them to the size you want.

You will also find "hibiscus trees" in the garden center. This is a pompom of leaves and flowers sitting atop a three or four foot trunk. Sometimes these are called standards, which is a nurseryman's term for a plant trained to tree form. Soon after you bring this little beauty home you will notice little green shoots sprouting all along the trunk and at the soil line. Understand that the plant is trying to develop into the form intended for it by nature, and that means a multi-stemmed shrub. If you want to keep it like a little tree you will need to constantly apply the shears.

Hibiscus aren't salt tolerant and they are the favorite salad green of several insects like aphids and white fly, but these are minor problems when you consider the beauty of the tropics bursting into bloom in your backyard.

Big Three of
Flowering Shrubs

Hibiscus

Camellia

Azalea

OTHER FLOWERING SHRUBS FOR FLORIDA

The options are overwhelming when it comes to selecting shrubs for your landscape. The following are a few lists of commonly available plants that aren't too demanding. We realize that your favorite may not be on the list, but a complete catalog of everything available would take volumes. Don't be shy about asking questions from your agricultural extension agent, local garden club or knowledgeable garden center staff.

FRAGRANT FLOWERING SHRUBS

Angel's trumpet	CS	Summer and autumn; white, peach or purple
Buddleia	CS	Midwinter, spring; lilac, white
Gardenia	NCS	Spring and early summer; white
Natal plum	CS	Most of the year; white flowers, red fruit
Night blooming jasmine	CS	Most of the year; white
Orange cestrum	CS	Warm months; yellow-orange
Orange jasmine	CS	Most of the year; white
Plumeria	CS	Warm months; many colors
Rose	NCS	All year (some seasonal); many colors

SNOWBIRD SPECIAL, WINTER BLOOMING SHRUBS

Allamanda	CS	Yellow, purple or pink
Azalea	NC	Red, pink and white
Buddleia	CS	Lilac, white (butterfly bush)
Calotropis	S	Purple or white (giant milkweed)
Camellia	NC	Red, pink and white
Hibiscus	CS	Many colors
Poinsettia	NCS	Red, pink or white
Powderpuff	CS	Red, pink or white (dwarf variety is everblooming)
Primrose jasmine	NC	Yellow flowers
Rose	NCS	Many colors

SALT TOLERANT FLOWERING SHRUBS

Bottlebrush	NCS	Somewhat tolerant
Buddleia	CS	Somewhat tolerant
Calotropis	S	Somewhat tolerant
Cereus peruvianus	NCS	Somewhat tolerant
Crown-of-thorns	CS	Very tolerant
Feijoa	NCS	Somewhat tolerant
Ixora	CS	Somewhat tolerant
Lantana	NCS	Very tolerant
Natal plum	CS	Very tolerant
Oleander	NCS	Very tolerant
Plumbago	CS	Somewhat tolerant
Plumeria	CS	Somewhat tolerant

DROUGHT TOLERANT FLOWERING SHRUBS

Beauty berry	NC
Bottlebrush	NCS
Crown-of-thorns	CS
Lantana	NCS
Oleander	NCS
Orange cestrum	CS
Plumeria	CS
Primrose jasmine	NC
Natal plum	C
Hedge cactus (Cereus peruvianus)	NCS

YES! YOU CAN GROW ROSES IN FLORIDA

Roses are sissies and wimps. Humidity, heat, too much water, not enough water, every insect in the state and susceptibility to every disease known to plants; all plague the poor hapless rose. We didn't even mention nematodes, did we? If it's this bad why do we bother trying to grow them?

True, we all enjoy complaining, and roses do give us lots to complain about, but it isn't as bad as it seems. First some good news, roses will grow and bloom all year long in all parts of Florida. They will do this for you in spite of all the pests and problems the gardening books delight in cataloguing.

While there are bugs down here, didn't you battle aphids, thrips, mites, mealy bugs and borers up north too? There is one pest you don't have to deal with here. You won't go into your garden some morning and find the flowers and leaves chewed into oblivion by Japanese beetles. They can't take the southern climate. Nor will you have to worry about winter protection, like those funny looking snow cones we used up there.

You may have to deal with downy mildew in January, but you can also take time to smell your home grown roses wearing shorts and a suntan. There aren't too many rose gardens in bloom in Michigan in January.

HERE ARE A FEW SUGGESTIONS TO HELP YOU GROW A SUCCESSFUL ROSE GARDEN IN FLORIDA

1. Roses do best in full sun. At least eight hours is a must for best bloom and compact growth. The sun also helps to control some of the fungus problems.

2. Roses need a rich well drained soil. They won't tolerate wet feet, but they do enjoy a soil rich in compost, sphagnum peat and composted cow manure. Mixing about two cups of bone meal per plant into the soil will encourage heavier bloom.

3. Before you plant work the organic matter into the soil to a depth of 18-20 inches. If you are setting out a large bed a roto-tiller will save you considerable time and energy. If you are planting a single plant work the compost into a space about two feet in diameter.

4. Don't water roses in the evening. When they go to bed with wet leaves they are much more likely to catch a fungus.

5. Prune out dead and weak canes and spent bloom. Gather and destroy fallen leaves. This also helps to avoid insects and disease.

6. Don't overfeed. This can encourage weak spindly growth that the bugs and fungi are particularly fond of.

7. Select your plants carefully when making the purchase. Make certain you are getting Florida grown stock.

8. Mulch heavily to control weeds, conserve moisture and keep the soil cool.

9. Consider installing a drip irrigation system. It is the least expensive watering system you can use and it conserves water.

10. Talk to members of a local garden club, your local agricultural extension office and knowledgeable garden center personnel.

HOW TO USE ROSES IN FLORIDA

Roses come in a variety of forms, colors and growth habits and while we usually picture roses in a formal rose garden they are far more versatile than that. Here are some suggestions on how you can use the most perfect of flowers.

1. One rose or a grouping can serve as an accent in front of a tree or large shrub, fountain, gazebo, arbor or park bench.

2. Don't be afraid to combine other plants like junipers, boxwood, serrisa, Mexican heather, Joseph's coat and a host of other materials as an edging for your roses.

3. Roses are fragrant. You can place a rose or two under a window and let the delightful scent follow the breezes into your home. Don't forget to perfume your Florida room, pool enclosure, etc. the same way.

4. Climbing roses can be trained against the side of a building, along the rails of a rustic fence as well as on the traditional trellis. They can make an informal screen.

5. Roses will grow well in containers if the pot is large enough and there is good drainage. This will permit moving the best blooming plant to the focal point and removing spent ones for refurbishing.

6. Miniature roses are easy and work well in hanging baskets, planters, window baskets, as an edging along walks and borders or as a ground cover in full sun.

SUCCESS WITH ROSES

You can grow beautiful fragrant roses in Florida, but success begins before you plant. Some of the experts recommend that you begin by cooking the soil in the planting site. You can do this by covering the area with clear plastic and sealing the edges with soil. Let the sun shine for a month or more. This will help to reduce the nematode population.

Work the organic matter mentioned above into the soil as deeply as you can. Don't worry about rose food or pesticides yet.

Select roses that are container grown in Florida. You aren't saving any money when you buy the bareroot or budget plants grown who knows where on unidentified rootstocks. Often promotional bareroot roses are offered that can't tolerate the heat or humidity in Florida and these plants, if they survive, will refuse to bloom.

ROOT STOCK is important. Most of the roses you find offered for sale are grafted. This means a bud from a named variety is spliced onto the seedling or rooted cutting of a variety that develops a strong root system suited to our sandy soil. Roses grown in Tennessee, Pennsylvania, Texas, California or most other states may be grafted onto root stocks that grow well in heavy clay soil or take freezing temperatures in stride, but they can't handle our soils, climate or pests well. Fortuniana and Dr. Huey are the most popular root stocks used in Florida, but some growers are using a special multiflora strain that has shown some promise in producing a deep root system that gets below the nematode zone.

There are hundreds of named varieties of roses. Many of these are recently developed and hold plant patents. Some of the best roses available today have also won awards from the American Rose Society. This isn't to say that some of the traditional roses, enjoyed for generations, aren't going to give you great bloom and a dependable plant. Double Delight, Garden Party, Mr. Lincoln, Angel Face and Peace are all non-patented roses now but all will perform well in this state.

Unfortunately many patented and non-patented roses don't respond well to our heat and humidity. This is another reason to invest in Florida grown stock. Often there will be poor bud formation, and flowers will have few petals. Some varieties that we grew quite well in the north will be susceptible to fungus and mildew problems in your Florida garden.

"BUY ROSES WHEN THEY ARE IN BLOOM" several of the rose growers told us when we asked them what advice they would give to someone new to Florida roses. There are several reasons for this.

1. First, you can see exactly what color bloom and flower form you are getting.

2. You can select a fragrance you like. Not all roses smell the same. Some are musky, others are spicy or have an old-fashioned rose scent. There are some roses that don't have much fragrance at all.

3. Remember that in Florida rose blooms will be larger in the cooler months when the buds take longer to form. Colors may also be different in winter months in some varieties.

4. "Look for healthy heavy canes arising from above the graft," was the advice given by another grower, "At least three husky canes are necessary to give you a prime plant."

5. Avoid plants that are showing leaf drop, have leaves that are dull, lackluster or peppered with black spots. New growth on a healthy rose is bright green or reddish in color, not yellow or pale green. Reading the rose leaves is one way to tell the plant's fortune. Bright shiny leaves indicate a long healthy life.

6. Avoid plants that have dried out or show signs of serious wilt. If they have been dry for a prolonged period of time serious root damage may have been done.

7. Never leave roses or any other plant in the car for more than a few minutes. In the Florida heat, even in the winter, the sun shines through a car window strong enough to raise the inside temperature to 120 degrees Fahrenheit. A few minutes at that temperature and you have parboiled rose leaves.

PLANTING ROSES

If you have prepared the site well by working lots of compost into the sandy soil the hard part has been done.

1. Water the plants and the site that is to be their new home.

2. Go inside and pour yourself a tall glass of iced tea, relax, read a couple more chapters of this book and wait at least an hour.

3. Now go back to your future rose garden, carefully remove the plant from the container and plant in the well prepared and moistened soil.

4. Plant so that the bud union (the knob just below where the canes start) is about an inch above the soil line. The depth it was growing in the container is usually about right.

5. Tamp the soil and soak well.

6. You can save yourself a lot of future effort if you now apply a weed block fabric and a mulch (or just mulch if you prefer). This will control weeds and conserve moisture.

7. You can now make a soil collar around each rose bush if you wish. This two foot ring will serve as a well to hold water so that it will soak in rather than run off. If you are using drip irrigation this isn't really necessary.

PROBLEMS YOU CAN HANDLE

Everyone complains about how hard roses are to grow and how many pests they have. You know what? They're right. Roses took a lot of extra effort in the northern climes too. The simple fact of the matter is that they are worth a little extra consideration. Sometimes we create our own problems with roses. The first line of defense is a strong healthy plant that is able to use its natural defenses to ward off insects and disease.

PREVENTIVE MEDICINE

1.   They need at least eight hours of sunshine every day. If you put your roses in partial shade they are going to be weak, spindly and lack the enthusiasm to bloom. Give them lots of sun.

2.   They can't stand wet feet so plant your roses where the soil is well drained.

3.   Roses need watering regularly and a drip irrigation system works extremely well for them. Try to avoid getting water on the leaves in the evening. This can encourage fungus and mildew.

4.   Avoid the temptation to overfeed. When roses are fed too much they become fat and lazy. The soft succulent branches are the favorite fare of a multitude of insects. Also, if too much nitrogen is fed to roses they will produce an enormous crop of leaves but few, if any, flowers.

5.   Review your rose garden weekly. Look on the underside of leaves for mites and insects. When these problems are spotted early they are easy to control. Prune off spent flower heads (the pros call this dead-heading), damaged twigs and canes and gather yellow or fallen leaves. This is the single most effective way to control disease.

6.   When you do prune, use sharp shears and make a clean angled cut. Try not to tear or leave ragged scars.

BUGS THAT LIKE YOUR ROSES MORE THAN YOU DO

Bugs are here to stay and while we tend to think of them as the enemy there are really only a few species that are antisocial by nature. Some of the ones you are likely to encounter in your rose garden are:

Aphids — they multiply rapidly and spend their time sucking the juices from the tender growth around new shoots and buds or the undersides of leaves. A minor infestation can be washed off with the garden hose. A more serious problem may require a mild pesticide, like an insecticidal soap, but the ladybug (beetle) is still the best control.

Scale is round off-white, gray or brown disc usually found massed on mature wood where they are gleefully sucking nutrients from the plant. The best offense here is to prune out infected wood but sometimes that isn't practical. There are many insecticides on the market that work well in controlling these critters.

Thrips are active little insects that hide in the center of buds and cause deformed flowers. Maintenance is your best defense. Dead-head weekly and if they become a problem use a good quality rose insecticide.

Spider mites are less than 1/50th of an inch long, but they devote their lives to only two pursuits, eating and multiplying. They are extremely good at both activities. The higher the temperature the faster they reproduce. When the temperature is in the eighties they can mature in less than a week. They establish colonies on the undersides of the leaves and in tents around buds. Here they can literally destroy a plant if not controlled. There are a number of good rose sprays on the market that can limit their damage, but maintenance is still the key. Clean up fallen leaves, watch closely and attack the colonies early.

Nematodes invade the roots and restrict the flow of water and nutrients to the plant. They cause nodules on the roots, but you don't see them until, in a fit of anger, you yank the dying plant from the soil. There is no really effective control for nematodes on established plants. Use plants grown on the Florida recommended root stocks and plant in soil rich in organic matter. In nematode prone areas solar sterilization (cooking the soil) can be helpful.

THE FUNGUS THAT ATE THE ROSE GARDEN

Disease is more insidious than insect infestation and can have more disastrous consequences. It is far easier to avoid these problems than to battle them. We discussed earlier the importance of keeping the roses healthy, growing in the sun and avoiding wet leaves. This is why.

Black spot is a fungus disease that shows itself as black spots or irregular patches on the leaves, often with a yellow edging to the spots. The leaf soon turns yellow and falls. The disease can be spread with a sprinkler system or spray from a hose. There are fungicides on the market that can be used, but follow the directions because a fungicide used improperly can do serious harm to the plant you are doctoring.

Downy mildew causes black lesions in the leaves and canes. It is most active in cool, wet weather and is difficult to control because it can spread from within the plant as well as on the surface. There are fungicides available that can help, but it is best controlled by pruning out and destroying the infected canes.

Powdery mildew is a disease that is active on the surface of the young leaves, new shoots and buds. What you see are the millions of spore clusters. If you can catch it early it can easily be controlled with a basic rose fungicide. Be certain to clean up fallen and infected leaves and destroy them. Powdery mildew is most common in warmer weather when there is high humidity.

We didn't list all these problems to scare you away from roses. The simple fact is they are not carefree plants. You will need to devote some time to them, but time spent in the rose garden is time well spent. Don't be afraid to clip bouquets of roses and bring into the house. Give some of the floral bounty to a neighbor, drop off a few at a local nursing home. Roses make people smile. Isn't that worth a little effort?

THE FENCE IS ALIVE, HEDGES

Hedges serve the same purpose as a fence, but somehow they seem friendlier. In the temperate clime you left behind hedges were used to define property lines, create boundaries, control foot traffic, frame the landscape, provide fragrance and color as well as provide a screen and cut noise pollution. Now that you are living in Florida the plant material is different, but the basic purpose and care of hedges is still the same.

We should warn you that hedges down here can suffer from starvation in a sandy soil that refuses to hold nutrients, and can become thirsty before you know it because sand doesn't hold water very well either. Fungus problems can hit a hedge that is too dense to permit proper air circulation, a cold snap following unseasonably warm winter weather can freeze tender growth. Oh, one more thing. The bugs are always hungry.

While it's true that fences need periodic painting and maintenance hedges aren't going to save you much labor. The Florida growing season is months longer than what you left "up there" so that more trimming and pruning are needed. A longer growing season means more feeding is required and there is the potential for more invasion of insects and disease. But don't despair, all is not lost. A lot of the hedge problems can be eliminated if you pay attention to three little phrases: plan ahead, prepare thoroughly, plant properly.

PLAN BEFORE YOU PURCHASE

Don't fall for a special sale price or a pretty flower. The super bargain may cost you in wasted labor and more money in the long run if it's the wrong plant material for your site.

1. First decide what you want the hedge to accomplish for you. Do you want a dense screen? Are you trying to attract birds? Is it a formal hedge or a low edging you are looking for?

2. You know where the hedge is going to be planted so the challenge for you is to find the right plant for those conditions. Don't be afraid to ask questions.

3. What is the sun-shade tolerance of the plants you are considering? Does this need match the amount of sunlight the site receives?

4. Can you satisfy the water needs of the plants you would like to plant there? Is irrigation possible, advisable or affordable?

5. Consider the cold hardiness your location dictates.

6. Is salt tolerance a factor?

7. Do you want the hedge to serve double duty by providing flowers, fragrance or fruit? A Florida hedge doesn't have to be just green. A hedge with thorns can also help create a secure barrier.

8. What size plants do you want to purchase? A hedge plant from a one gallon container will be the same size as one from a three gallon pot in a few short months. The smaller starting size is also a lot easier for you to handle, and there is less chance of transplanting shock.

9. What are the advantages of a given species, what are its disadvantages? Learn all you can about the varieties available before you trade cash for your final selection. Don't be afraid to ask questions. Before you decide, get some advice from your local extension office, garden center personnel or garden club. Don't be hesitant to visit your local library for information as well.

10. Use the following lists as a starting point in your selection.

FAST GROWING HEDGES

Ligustrum (Privet)	NCS
Cherry laurel	NC
Photinia, red tip	NC
Silverthorn	NC
Hibiscus	CS
Oleander	NCS
Poinciana shrub	CS
Viburnum sandankwa	NC
Sweet viburnum	NCS
Powderpuff	CS

DROUGHT TOLERANT

Ligustrum (Privet)	NCS
Wax myrtle	NCS
Photinia, red tip	NC
Silverthorn	NC
Boxwood	NC
Oleander	NCS
Natal plum	CS
Glossy abelia	NC
Sweet viburnum	NCS
Viburnum sandankwa	NCS

SALT TOLERANT

Wax myrtle	NCS
Pittosporum	NCS
Indian hawthorn	NC
Yaupon holly	NC
Silverthorn	NC
Oleander	NCS
Natal plum	CS
Podocarpus	NCS

FORMAL STYLE HEDGE

Podocarpus	NCS
Cherry laurel	NC
Ligustrum (privet)	NCS
Japanese boxwood	NC
Japanese holly	N
Chinese holly	NC
Natal plum	CS
Photinia	NC

LOW HEDGE (under 3')

Azaleas, some var.	NC
Many junipers	NC
Crimson barberry	NC
Indian hawthorn	NC
Holly malpighia	S
Boxwoods	NC
Dwarf hollies	NC
Natal plum	CS
Glossy abelia	NC

TALL INFORMAL HEDGE (over 8')

Podocarpus	NCS
Wax myrtle	NCS
Cherry laurel	NC
Photinia	NC
Ligustrum (privet)	NCS
Yaupon holly	NC
Camellia	NC
Silverthorn	NC
Oleander	NCS
Bush cherry	CS
Viburnums	NC

FLOWERING HEDGES

Azalea	NC	Winter and spring
Cherry laurel	NC	Early spring; white flowers
Indian hawthorn	NC	Spring and early summer; pink flowers
Powderpuff	CS	Winter and spring;red flowers
Orange jasmine	CS	Fragrant white flowers and red berries most of the year
Holly malpighia	S	Pink flowers, red fruit all year
Camellia	NC	Fall and winter bloom
Glossy abelia	NC	White flowers all summer
Oleander	NCS	Blooms throughout warm months
Barbados fence flower (Poinciana pulcherrima)	S	Scarlet and yellow flowers throughout warm months
Hibiscus	CS	Everblooming
Rose of Sharon	NC	Northern cousin of hibiscus, blooms throughout warm months

HEDGE PLANTS WITH THORNS FOR SECURITY

Barberry	NC	Crimson pygmy makes great low hedge or border
Boxthorn	CS	Dense thorny cousin to orange
Calamondin orange	NCS	Fragrant flowers; takes pruning well
Chinese holly	NC	Effective, formal or informal
Firethorn (Pyracantha)	NC	White flowers in spring, red berries in winter
Hedge cactus (Cereus peruvianus)	NCS	Beautiful flowers, trouble-free
Lime berry	S	Fragrant white flowers, red berries on 6 foot cousin of orange
Prickly pear cactus	NCS	Many varieties; most effective barrier

PREPARE THE SITE BEFORE YOU PURCHASE THE PLANTS

Deciding what species or variety of plant you want for a hedge is only the first step. Now you need to roll up your sleeves and get to work.

1. The first step is to measure the area and mark with stakes and string exactly where the hedge is going.

2. You know the hedge is going to grow so hold it back from the property line. It doesn't promote friendly relations with the neighbors when your landscape crowds out their grass or flower border. There are also often local ordinances that regulate the distance from the property line you can plant.

3. If the hedge line is lengthy you may want to rent a roto-tiller to clear all the existing vegetation. Some prefer to use a universal weed killer like Round-Up and wait a week or two to plant. Either way, the weeds need to be removed.

4. Work compost or other organic matter into the soil as deeply as you can. About four to six inches of compost worked into the top twelve to fifteen inches of the soil will do wonders for your future hedge. A roto-tiller is helpful here too.

5. If you are going to lay irrigation lines for a sprinkler system now is the time to do it. If drip irrigation is your choice it can be installed after the planting is done.

6. Determine the proper spacing and how many plants you will need.

7. Select the plants that appear to be the most healthy. Avoid spindly, weak or dull colored plants. There is no need to bring home problems. Compact, well branched plants make the best choice.

8. Don't make a big deal about them all being the same size when you select them at the nursery. You can always prune them all to the same height and width when you get them home.

9. Water the plants and the planting site well at least an hour or two before planting.

10. Avoid planting during the hottest part of the day. This is hard on you and doesn't do the plants too much good either.

PLANTING IS THE EASY PART

If you have prepared the site properly and you follow these suggestions you will be amazed at how easily a trunk full of plants becomes a hedge.

1. Dig the holes at the proper intervals and use the string to make certain they are in a straight line.

2. Remove from the nursery can and plant at the same depth. Many of the common hedge plants have surface feeder roots and if they are planted deeper than they were grown they will literally suffocate.

3. Be careful not to let the roots dry out at any time during the planting process.

4. After all the plants have been set out water thoroughly and tamp the soil down with your heel to eliminate any possible air pockets.

5. Stretch the string at a suitable height and prune all the plants accordingly. Now they are all starting off equal. Future prunings will keep the energetic ones in check and a little extra feeding can encourage the reluctant ones to catch up.

6. Now you can spread a weed block material and/or a couple inches of mulch to help conserve moisture and control weeds.

7. You can use a starter solution but it isn't necessary. It is best to wait until there is some new top growth to start your regular feeding program.

8. Water two or three times a week until well established.

9. There will often be a plant or two that doesn't seem to grow with the same enthusiasm the rest of them display. This is usually because the sprinkler doesn't hit them as well as it does the others. It can also be caused by heavier shade cast on part of the hedge from buildings or neighboring trees.

After the hedge is established and it has become a part of the landscape you will still have to climb out of the pool or leave the comfortable chairs in the Florida room and do some maintenance. Remember, this is Florida. There is no snow to shovel, but that means the weeds still grow, the bugs still bite and the plants tend to get unruly. Frequent pruning throughout the growing season is easier than waiting until there is a major landscaping overhaul needed.

Try to avoid making the most common mistake with hedges. That's letting them grow without any guidance because you want them to reach the desired height as soon as possible. Then you spend a lot of time complaining about how open and downright ugly the hedge looks. Prune frequently. It encourages denser growth and a fuller plant.

Prune flowering hedges soon after a blooming cycle has been completed. Waiting too long results in eliminating the next season's flowers. For example, trimming azaleas in September means you've probably chopped off more than half of the next winter's flowers.

VINES FOR RAPID GROWTH

Vines have been described as weak wimpy shrubs that can't stand on their own; yet they are eager to fill in the blank spots in your landscape, and the chances are they can do it quicker than anything else you can plant. Whether it's bare soil in need of a ground cover, an arbor that would be more inviting with some shade or a fence that needs softened with some color there is a vine ready and waiting to fill the need.

To many professional landscapers vines are the outcasts of the residential grounds. Perhaps it's because they grow with an enthusiasm that's difficult to control, or maybe it's because they'll grow quite well without your help; either way they're the forgotten part of the Florida landscape. Not all vines are like kudzu, the plant that ate the south. You remember the clematis that delicately graced your trellis in Ohio? In Florida we have dozens of different colors and shapes of passion vine. Some of your old friends are here too, like wisteria, honeysuckle, Virginia creeper and trumpet vine.

Vines can serve you well as a fast growing rugged screen where a solid wood fence looks too stark or unfriendly. On an arbor well chosen vines can cast a comforting shade. Vines can produce exotic fragrances like chalice vine or the jasmines. A spindly palm can be fleshed out with a vine or two planted at it's base. Don't forget the value of vines in containers where they can drape over walls or cascade from a hanging basket. Where shade discourages grass there are many vines that will eagerly serve as ground covers. Some vines, like the kiwi, cucumbers, chayote and some of the passionfruit, produce edible fruit as well as pretty flowers.

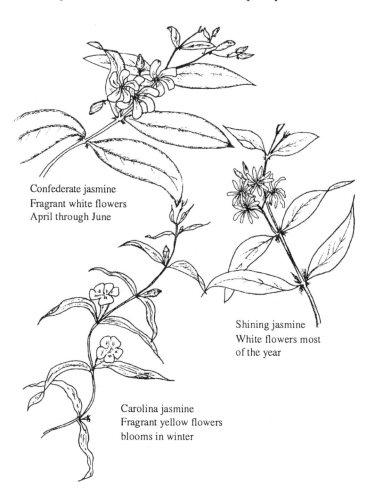

Confederate jasmine
Fragrant white flowers
April through June

Shining jasmine
White flowers most
of the year

Carolina jasmine
Fragrant yellow flowers
blooms in winter

Passion Vine

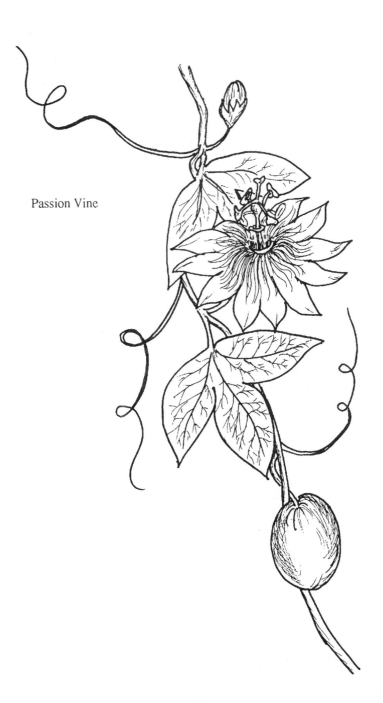

The following are only a few suggestions. This is by no means a complete list of all the vines you can grow in Florida. We would also like to note that while we make recommendations for N - north, C - central and S - south Florida, there is always the possibility of growing an extremely frost sensitive plant in a container throughout the state. Don't be afraid to experiment.

WOODY VINES FOR COLOR ON A FENCE		
Bougainvillea	CS	Many colors, many seasons
Carolina jasmine	NC	Yellow flowers in winter
Confederate jasmine	NCS	White flowers spring and early summer
Pandora vine	CS	Pink flowers in spring
Bleeding heart (Clerodendrum)	NCS	White and red flowers in clusters
Coral vine (Antigonon)	NCS	Clusters of pink or white flowers
Japanese honeysuckle	NC	White and cream flowers all year
Painted trumpet	NCS	Large lavender flowers in spring
Passion vine	NCS	Many colors, different seasons
Rangoon creeper	S	White flowers that turn pink
Trumpet honeysuckle	NC	Florida native; red flowers all year
Queen's wreath	S	Substitute for wisteria in south Florida

VINES THAT GROW WELL IN SHADE	
Philodendron	CS
Creeping fig	NCS
Grape ivy	S
English ivy	NCS
Kangaroo vine	S
Virginia creeper	NC

VINES FOR GROUND COVER	
English ivy	NCS
Grape ivy	S
Mexican flame vine	CS
Wedelia	CS
Asiatic jasmine	NCS
Confederate jasmine	NCS
Creeping fig	NCS
Honeysuckle	NC
Sweet potato	NCS

ANNUAL VINES FOR COLOR AND COVER ON TRELLIS, FENCE OR ARBOR	
Black-eyed susan vine	Gourds
Canary vine	Moonvine
Cardinal flower	Morning glory

VINES WITH FRAGRANT BLOOM		
Carolina jasmine	NC	Yellow flowers in winter
Chalice vine	S	Flowers open white, turn gold; fragrance of coconut
Confederate jasmine	NCS	White flowers; the jasmine you came to Florida for
Herald's trumpet	CS	Huge white flowers; very fragrant
Japanese honeysuckle	NC	Traditional fragrance

MASSIVE VIGOROUS VINES		
Monstrosa	S	Split leaf three feet long, like philodendron
Rangoon creeper	S	Will outgrow almost any other vine
Herald's trumpet	S	Heavy vine that requires support
Chalice vine	CS	Heavy vine that requires support

Most of the vines listed here are not too demanding as to soil needs. Generally a well drained site where compost or other organic matter has been worked into the soil is all they ask. Be cautious in feeding these vines because too much of a good thing will diminish flowering and increase the rampant growth. Don't be afraid to prune heavily and often. Most of the vines listed here have few insect or fungus problems and cold damage is only a temporary setback. Vines create an informal natural look that is relaxed and comfortable. They can also help to support beneficial birds and lizards that eat insects.

Some claim vines need a great deal of maintenance, but this isn't always the case. While many vines may need more frequent pruning than some other plant forms they generally require less feeding, disease and insect control. If you are a winter resident don't neglect this potential. The rugged nature of most vines makes them valuable in a landscape that must fend for itself for part of the year.

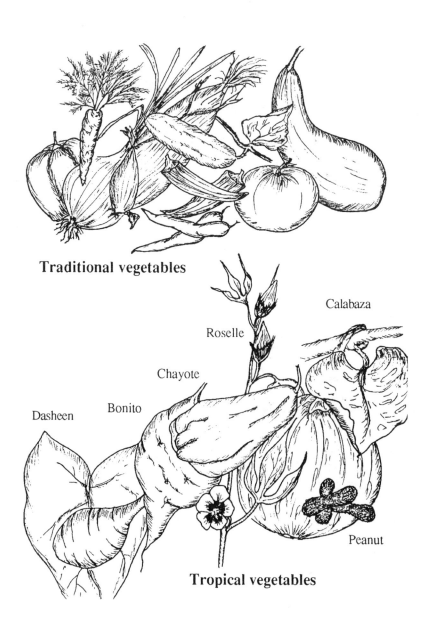

Traditional vegetables

Calabaza

Roselle

Chayote

Dasheen   Bonito

Peanut

Tropical vegetables

SECTION SIX

WHAT'S FOR DINNER?

THE TWELVE MONTH SALAD BOWL

It used to be so easy. When we lived "up there" all we had to do was follow our instincts. At the first signal that spring would come again the primal urge to till the earth awakened within us. That sign often occurred in early January with a trip to the mailbox. Remember when you waded through slush and snow, but it was worth it because there was a mail order seed catalog waiting for you?

Armed with this a good Yankee gardener could, at will, transport himself into the vegetable patch of the future. Gazing out the frost-covered window at the now dismal gray of a winter that had overstayed its welcome, the Yankee could see rows of lacy carrot leaves and sweet corn coming into tassel. Bushels of vine ripened tomatoes symbolized a bountiful harvest. There was even a hint of danger as our Yankee gardener looked into the future at the zucchini vines that never sleep. Zucchini is our Yankee answer to the southern kudzu vine. In your mind you see these demon vines. They have escaped and carpeted the driveway, eaten the carport and are now invading the neighbor's rose garden.

Wake up! You ain't in Ohio anymore. You're in Florida and the vegetable gardening game is played by different rules here. If you employ many of the tricks and techniques that made you a blue ribbon gardener at the country fair in Wisconsin you might be doomed to haunting the produce counter at the local supermarket here.

The first rule is that there is no time off for good behavior in the Florida vegetable garden. Up there we got to relax all winter and dine on the produce we had put by, stored, canned, frozen, pickled, dried or in some other way preserved. Here you can grow tomatoes in the middle of winter, in fact much of the garden does better in the winter when the heat is less oppressive. There is something happening every month in the Florida veggie patch.

The second difference is that the biggest problems are too small to be seen. In our gardens in the north the threats to our backyard agriculture included caterpillars, beetles and other pests. While we have them here too, the problems that are life threatening to our plants are often microscopic. What you see are the effects of nematodes, molds, fungi, mildews and virus diseases, not the little demons themselves.

The third rule of thumb for Yankees gardening in this state is to give up on trying to grow the following unless you like a real challenge. Most of these can be grown in northern or central Florida, but it takes extra effort and the results are usually far from spectacular.

Asparagus
Artichokes
Broad beans (fava beans need cooler weather)
Brussels sprouts (will go to seed before a good crop is produced)
Many cabbage varieties (there are some good Florida varieties)
Swiss chard (poor leaf quality)
Head lettuce
Horseradish
Many potatoes (some Florida varieties give a good crop)
Rhubarb

The fourth rule for Florida gardening is to work and water in the early morning hours soon after sunrise. Mosquitoes are less active and it is cooler so there is less strain on you. Watering done early in the day is less likely to result in the spread of fungus disease, plus the plants are better able to handle the stress from the bright Florida sun after they have had a cool drink.

BIG DECISIONS IN THE VEGETABLE GARDEN

It's up to you whether you want a massive garden with space for a tractor to drive up and down the rows or a more modest intensive gardening plot. For most of us Yankees the intensive gardening style is more appropriate. This lets you companion plant, rotate crops, control the composition of the soil and conserve water. Not to mention that it takes a lot less sweat per bowl of salad produced.

A big garden wastes a lot of space and requires more labor, pesticide, fertilizer and water. We have seen small, well planned plots produce many times more in a year's time than a full size garden that covered far more area.

By planting in groups and solid beds rather than rows, yield per area is increased. Intercropping (planting a rapidly maturing plant like radishes with slower developing vegetables such as cucumbers) makes for efficient use of limited space. When the first is harvested room is left for the other to grow and mature. By companion planting (growing two compatible plants like corn and beans together) you can get even greater harvests.

Intensive gardening also crowds out the weeds so that there is less effort needed to keep the beds pest free.

You can make your work even easier if you build raised beds by using concrete block, landscape timbers or railroad ties to create a frame. Then fill them with compost and top soil. This provides a controlled growing medium for the plants and less stooping for you.

Pests in the soil can be combated before planting, but little is effective after the veggies have moved in. You can use a soil fumigant, but these chemicals are highly toxic and some are restricted to professional use. There are organic materials on the market made from pulverized sea shells and other materials that show some promise as a nematode control, but there is something you can do that costs almost nothing and kills a lot of the weed seeds and insect pests as well as nematodes. Bake the soil in a solar oven. All you need to do is moisten the soil and spread a piece of clear plastic (black reflects the heat and it doesn't get as hot underneath). cover the edges with soil to seal it and wait about four weeks. There is only one catch here. The soil needs to be in full sun, but then, so should your garden.

You can also help discourage pests by planting some of the stuff the bugs don't like in with your vegetables. Many beetles and aphids refuse to dine where garlic and chives are growing. Some experts use dwarf marigolds to beat nematodes into submission and ornamental hot peppers to discourage some snails and slugs.

A lot of disease and insect problems can be avoided by planting the newer varieties that are resistant to the pests. Many tomatoes, melons and beans are almost immune to some of the most common virus and bacterial problems. This can save you a lot of expense, labor and disappointment.

How to water is another decision you will have to make, because in Florida it is guaranteed that you will have to provide water to grow vegetables successfully. For most homeowners irrigation ditches are out of the question, but sprinkler systems and drip irrigation are labor saving answers to hand watering. Drip systems are inexpensive and easy to install plus they use far less water.

One other way to water more efficiently is what we refer to as the Lay's potato chip method of gardening, i.e. with ruffles and ridges. For plants that need a lot of water you can create ridges or walls along the rows to prevent wasteful runoff. For plants that can't tolerate wet feet you can plant on top of slightly elevated ridges. Strawberries respond well to this ridgetop residence.

GARDENING IN FLORIDA IS A MATTER OF TIMING

Yankees have the most difficulty in vegetable gardening here because they try to follow the same planting and harvest schedule we did in the north. We suggest that you pay a visit to your local agricultural extension office and pick up a copy of their seasonal planting chart and the latest information on the newest varieties. They are the experts, they have spent years studying Florida crops and test planting both new and traditional varieties. Following the advice they provide will go a long way towards achieving a successful harvest.

One of the other problems we Yankees have when we come down here is that we want to grow the same crops and varieties here we grew up there. While many of them will grow quite well here others are not suitable and there is also a wealth of southern varieties of northern plants that know how to handle the pests and problems down here. Take tomatoes as an example. Homestead, Floramerica and Tropired are reliable growers here, but you would be disappointed with their performance in New York state. Use varieties that are recommended for your area. Your local agricultural extension office can help you here.

One of the mistakes we often make with vegetables is assuming that they have to be grown in a vegetable garden. Many tomatoes can be grown in containers, there are even cucumbers that will accept pot culture well. Strawberries work well as a ground cover or in a hanging basket. Don't ignore the landscape potential of these edibles.

SOME SOUTHERN DELIGHTS
YOU COULDN'T GROW UP THERE

One of the joys of vegetable gardening in Florida is that you can experience the thrill of growing some new and different plants. Because we can experience a touch of the tropics we can grow beyond the basic southern crops like okra and cow peas and include cassava, chayote, Malabar spinach and so much more. The following is only the start if you want to grow exotic fruits and vegetables.

AMARANTH (tampala) The seed for this tropical American vegetable is difficult to find but it is worth the effort. It thoroughly enjoys the summer heat and provides a continuous source of leaves for fresh salads.

BONITA (Cuban sweet potato) This is a white version of the common sweet potato. It is a member of the morning glory family and thrives with little care in Florida's sandy soil.

CASSAVA This is the source of tapioca. The six to eight foot shrub has attractive finely cut leaves. The roots are harvested for a flour and tapioca. Processing this can be an interesting family experience. The plants are often found in your local garden center.

CHAYOTE is the fruit of a Central American vine that will overrun trees or your porch if given the chance. It can be easily started by planting the whole fruit stem end up in compost enriched soil. The fruit matures in the fall and winter. It may freeze to the ground, but will come back with a vengeance. The fruit is great sliced raw in a salad, fried or prepared a number of other ways.

COLLARDS is sometimes referred to as wild cabbage. In reality it is a cabbage that doesn't know how to form a head. It grows easily from seed and is best in the cool months although it can be grown in the summer. There are more insect problems in the warm months however.

COW PEAS are also called southern peas. This is so they won't be confused with the peas we grew up north which they call garden peas or English peas down here. Cow peas are a warm season crop and grow with little difficulty. They can be harvested as green beans or left to dry on the plant and shelled. Either way they are delightful. There are many colorful varieties like the famous black-eyed pea.

CUBAN PUMPKIN or calabaza is the Cuban answer to the zucchini. All you have to do is plant it and get out of the way. It will grow 40 to 60 feet and climb over anything that gets in its way, including trees, parked cars and small children. The round green, cream and yellow fruit usually weighs 6-10 pounds. The flavor is somewhat different than squash, but they are delightful baked.

DASHEEN, TARO, EDDO AND YAUTIA are all root crops from the same plant family that brought you elephant ears, caladiums and jack-in-the-pulpit. In many areas of the south and all of the Caribbean they are a valuable cash crop. The tubers are higher in protein than white potatoes and the flavor is almost nut like. You can purchase small ones in the supermarket and plant them in compost enriched soil. Not only do they willingly produce a good crop for you, they provide attractive foliage as well.

GINGER is more properly a spice than a vegetable, but it is still something that you can grow in your Florida garden so we are including it here. You can purchase a couple fresh tubers at the supermarket and plant them in compost enriched soil that can be kept moist. They will form an attractive clump of foliage and white or greenish-cream flowers. You can harvest the fresh ginger in the fall and replant some to grow again. It makes a great novelty plant to impress the visitors from back home.

MALABAR SPINACH is a succulent vine that is great in a salad. Both leaves and stems are tender and tasty. The seed is offered in many specialty seed catalogs. They grow quite easily trained on a wire or trellis. A few plants will keep the salad bowl full all summer long.

MUSTARD GREENS may taste a little bitter to some, but it's a flavor that grows on you. They are almost too easy to grow and mature in 40 to 45 days. Mustard is at its best as a cool season crop.

OKRA is an edible member of the hibiscus family. The flavor of the young seed pods is delicious no matter how you prepare them. They grow easily from seed and mature in 50 to 60 days. This is a great warm season crop.

PEANUTS are members of the bean family and, like many of the other southern produce plants, are attractive in foliage and flower. The mound of green leaves is dotted with the yellow flowers. After pollination the flower stem drops over to the ground and the seedpod, what we call the peanut, forms in the soil. They work well as an edging or in a flower border.

ROSELLE, sometimes called the Florida cranberry, is a member of the hibiscus family. It is an annual plant maturing at 4 to 7 feet with attractive reddish green foliage and cream colored hibiscus shaped flowers. The young leaves and stems add a dash of tartness to a salad, but they are usually grown for the red colored calyx behind the flower. This is used to make sauces and jellies. It's a warm weather vegetable that also doubles as an attractive background plant in the flower border.

WINGED BEAN is one of those botanical wonders. You can eat the flowers, leaves, young fruit and mature seed pods. This vining member of the legume family is easy to grow in all parts of Florida and can take the place of sweet peas because it willingly produces quantities of lavender blue flowers. Prune it back frequently to encourage dense growth and fill the salad bowl.

YUCCA produces an edible root that can be processed into a flour or cooked like a potato. In our taste testing this was not one of the winners, but it still has novelty value.

WHEN TO PLANT YOUR FLORIDA GARDEN

Everyone that writes a book on Florida vegetable gardening uses these lengthy and detailed charts that the University of Florida has produced after years of research. You can pick up a copy of this free at your local agricultural extension office so we aren't going to reprint it here. We do want to distinguish between the two types of Yankee gardeners that inhabit this state though. If you are what the natives affectionately refer to as a "snowbird," defined as a winter resident, you are going to want to cultivate a different garden than the full time resident who lives and works (or is retired) here. Those in this latter category have the opportunity to see a garden plot produce unbelievable amounts of vegetables because it never rests.

With many of the vegetables we can grow here the true Florida advantage is that you can get a double harvest. Let's face it. You can plant tomatoes in the fall and harvest them while the relatives you left behind are scraping ice from their windshields, then you can plant again in the spring and enjoy bacon, lettuce and tomato sandwiches this summer too.

With some plants like mustard greens, collards and beans the harvest can be almost continuous. By spacing plantings a couple weeks apart fresh beets, carrots, radishes, onions, even peppers and cucumbers can also be enjoyed much of the year.

Because you can rotate crops and gain multiple harvests it is wise to avoid overdoing the garden. Don't plant more space than you can comfortably handle. After all this is supposed to be relaxation, not punishment. We do suggest also that surplus produce makes a great neighborly gift and there are numerous food banks in this state that can put what you don't need to good use.

VEGETABLES THE WINTER RESIDENTS
CAN PLANT WHEN YOU GET HERE

There may be some cold weather restrictions in the northern part of the state.

Beets	Broccoli	Cabbage
Carrots	Cauliflower	Chinese cabbage
Endive	Kohlrabi	Lettuce
Lima beans	Mustard	Onions
Parsnips	Peas, English or garden type	Peppers, sweet and hot
Pole beans	Potatoes (S. Fla)	Snap beans
Spinach	Squash	Strawberry
Sweet corn (S. Fla)	Tomatoes	Turnips

Spring unofficially begins the day after Christmas in Florida and a lot of gardening can be done in January and February.

After the serious threat of freezing weather is over you can plant such crops as cantaloupe, cucumbers, corn, watermelon and southern peas. This early spring season is also an ideal time to plant a second crop of most of the vegetables listed above.

Some of the experts say you get to take summer off in the Florida garden, but you can still plant beans, southern peas, okra and many of the tropical crops mentioned earlier in this chapter. The subtropical summers here can give you a whole different world of gardening, and fill your salad bowl with exotic fruits and vegetables you never saw in the northern supermarkets.

ORANGE BLOSSOM SYNDROME

The orange tree is the transplanted Yankee's declaration of independence from snow, ice and the other joys of winter "up there." It also has a place in the hearts of native Floridians. It's their apple, one of their state's major industries; the orange is a true Florida institution. If you are going to claim residence in this state it is only right that some member of this vast and varied citrus family be invited into your backyard.

Wait a minute! Why did we say backyard? Why should this king of Florida fruit trees be tucked away in the back corner of the lot? Why do we assume there is this segregation of produce and utility out back, while the more visible front is reserved for functionless beauty, plantings for show only? Let's rethink this custom and try giving these versatile trees a shot at the limelight. An orange or grapefruit tree planted near the screen room or near open windows will fill the house with its unique and delightful fragrance. This perfume alone is a good enough reason to move to Florida.

Not only do citrus provide floral beauty, fragrance and healthy produce, they also offer rich green foliage on a tree that willingly accepts pruning and shaping. Citrus do well in central and south Florida, but north of Ocala most varieties run afoul of the cold weather. This isn't cause for despair though because many members of the family do quite well in containers and will bear a good crop even if they reside in a portable grove.

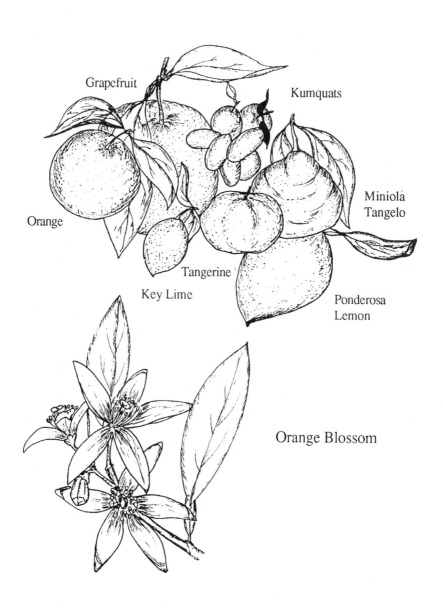

Grapefruit

Kumquats

Orange

Miniola
Tangelo

Tangerine

Key Lime

Ponderosa
Lemon

Orange Blossom

SOME SUGGESTIONS ON CITRUS TO PLANT

GRAPEFRUIT — Home harvested grapefruit have a special flavor and most varieties mature over a long period of time between November and May. Unlike the apples and pears you grew up north grapefruit do not require cross pollination.

DUNCAN is the old standard and is the most cold hardy, but it has lots of seeds.

MARSH WHITE bears well and is seedless.

THOMPSON PINK is the most common seedless pink flesh.

RUBY RED is a popular seedless red flesh.

There are dozens of other varieties that are excellent as well.

ORANGES are the major citrus crop in Florida and the Valencia accounts for about half the commercial production. While there are dozens of varieties that will do well in your home grove the following are some varieties that are most popular.

NAVEL oranges are familiar to everyone. They are seedless, have a great sweet flavor, low acid content and are great for juice as well as eating. They are harvested between November and February.

TEMPLE oranges are excellent for eating or juice, almost seedless and a bit more acidic than navels. They can be picked between January and March.

VALENCIA is a seedless sweet orange that is great for juice or eating. If you live here year round and can give a good home to only one orange tree this is probably your best choice. It, like most citrus, stores well on the tree and provides a healthy treat from March through June.

HAMLIN in one of the traditional dooryard citrus fruits. It's seedless, sweet and peels easily. Like most oranges it is good for both juice and eating. It's another early season orange, maturing from October to January.

PINEAPPLE is another of the old standard oranges that Floridians have been growing for generations. It has a good flavor, but some object to its seeds. It's supposedly the most widely grown orange in Florida. It is considered a mid-season orange because it ripens from December to February.

PARSON BROWN is the third of the best kept secrets of the native Floridians. A great sweet flavor, but again some object to the seeds. It's a dependable orange though and has the longest harvest season of all the oranges. it matures from October through March, but can be stored on the tree until May.

TANGERINES are some of the best citrus for eating out of hand and most varieties also make a delightful juice too. They are generally more cold hardy and can extend the range of citrus into northern Florida. Some of the varieties that are classified as tangerines the consumer considers oranges, but a tangerine by any other name is just as sweet.

DANCY is what everyone thinks of when tangerines are mentioned. This is that rich deep orange color, loose skin and segments that separate easily. This is the Christmas tangerine that is harvested in December and January. It's the most common of the tangerines.

MURCOTT (HONEY ORANGE) is our personal favorite because it combines low acid with the sweetest flavor of all the tangerines. It looks more like an orange than a tangerine, but there is a good reason. The Murcott is a hybrid. Its mamma was a tangerine, but its daddy was an orange. It's very cold hardy and matures between the navel and the valencia, January through April.

SATSUMA is another of the extremely hardy tangerines that looks like an orange. If space is a factor it has a compact growth habit and will be quite happy in a large container in areas where cold weather is a reality. It's an excellent choice for the homeowner because it is a fall citrus, you can harvest between September and November.

ROBINSON is another tangerine that looks like we expect a tangerine to look. With loose skin, deep orange color and lots of seeds. It's cold hardy and gives you tangerines a couple months before Dancy.

TANGELOS are a cross between tangerines and oranges and carry on some of the best traits of each of their parents. From the tangerine they got greater cold tolerance and a skin that's easy to peel. From the orange they got increased size, fewer seeds and a longer storage life.

MINNEOLA (HONEY BELL) produces a medium to large sized fruit that often has a neck and resembles a bell. It has a very sweet flesh with only a few seeds. It is extremely cold hardy and gives a dependable crop from December until late April.

ORLANDO is the most widely grown tangelo in Florida. It is often used as a pollinator for other citrus. It is also one of the most cold hardy citrus fruits.

LEMONS and LIMES are more the province of southern Florida, but they can be grown in the rest of the state with winter protection or container culture.

PONDEROSA LEMON is a lemon that some claim looks like a yellow football. It is larger than some grapefruit and underneath the thick skin is enough juice to make a pitcher of lemonade from a single fruit. They also make an excellent marmalade and a great pie. On the plus side, they are everbearing and will provide their haunting floral fragrance all year long if— and this is the down side— they don't get a chill. They are very cold sensitive.

MEYER LEMON is also everbearing and is cold hardy throughout most of central Florida. It has a lower acidity than most other lemons and makes the best juice.

KEY LIMES are legendary in Florida. What grits is to Georgia, key lime pie is to Florida. We think of limes as green, but the key lime is yellow when ripe. Its talent goes beyond the pie shell, however. Try some, squeeze it yourself, fresh lime juice. It's almost reason enough to move to Florida. It's also cold sensitive and whimpers at the weatherman's mention of low temperatures. Key limes do make great container plants though and will bear well. They are everbearing with the heaviest crop from September to December.

PERSIAN LIMES look like a traditional lime is supposed to look, small and green. This is the lime you often find in the supermarket. They are also cold sensitive. You can pick Persian limes from June through September.

KUMQUATS are not a joke played on unsuspecting newcomers to the state. They exist, and as far as we are concerned they are a gourmet food. Think about it. This is Florida's answer to cherries. They are a miniature orange that you eat skin and all. They are great as a marmalade, in a pie or candied. Kumquats ripen from November through May, but they will often bloom and bear out of season. They are more a shrub than a tree and can be trained to shape, grown in a container or used as a hedge. They are quite cold hardy and are worth considering for your landscape.

MEIWA KUMQUATS are round while **NEGAME KUMQUATS** are oval shaped. Both are delicious, fragrant and make an attractive shrub.

CALAMONDIN ORANGE is the miniature orange tree the tourists buy in little cardboard boxes to take home and put on their windowsill. Here they make an impressive, not so dwarf, tree (15 to 25 feet) that can be sheared into a hedge. The fruit is bitter, but makes a good marmalade.

FINDING JUST THE RIGHT SPOT TO PLANT YOUR NEWLY PURCHASED CITRUS

Whenever anyone moves to Florida, before they start newspaper delivery, before they apply for the homestead exemption, long before they take the test for the Florida driver's license, they succumb to the disease called "the orange blossom syndrome" and buy an orange tree. They bring it home and sit it in the middle of the driveway, study it and take a few photos of the family gathered around it (these are sent to relatives and friends left behind in the north). Then they carry it all over the yard looking for the perfect spot to plant it. When the citrus bug bites here are some suggestions to help you and your orange tree enjoy a happy relationship.

1.   A sunny spot is best, but sunshine at least 50% of the day is a must if you want more than a few struggling branches.

2.   The soil must be well drained, but there must be water available.

3.   Avoid problems. Keep citrus, and most other trees and shrubs, away from septic tanks and drains.

4.   Keep the trees at least 15 to 25 feet from the house, buildings and other large trees. The tree may look like a twig in a three gallon pot today, but it will grow up. Most citrus trees will form a crown spread ranging from 12 to 15 feet.

5.   Don't be afraid to use a citrus as a landscape tree. It combines beautiful fragrant flowers with a well behaved growth habit. Any citrus can be pruned to conform to most of the demands your landscape might make. On a small lot it may be a better choice than a massive oak or slash pine.

HOW TO PLANT AN ORANGE TREE

Every text you read goes through this involved planting procedure with pages of dire warnings, cautions and don't you dares. It's enough to make you give up and visit the fruit market when you want a grapefruit. Fear not! If you can come close to following these suggestions you will be drinking your own home grown orange juice next year.

1. Work some compost or other organic matter into the soil and dig a hole twice as wide and just as deep as the container in which the tree was grown. The organic matter encourages the roots to be adventurous and explore beyond the root mass that came out of the container.

2. Remove the root mass from the container and carefully spread some of the fibrous roots if it looks overly potbound. Be careful not to break them.

3. Place in the hole so that the graft (bud union) is above the soil line. Usually the depth it was growing at while in the container is about right.

4. Fill in around the root mass with the compost enriched soil and water. Pack the soil with your heel and water again. This will help avoid air pockets and dry roots.

5. Now comes the part that makes you look like a pro. Make a ring of soil about four feet in diameter around the trunk. This collar should be about four inches high. Now fill this reservoir with water.

6. Water two, maybe three times a week by filling this little pond to the brim. Avoid the temptation to water every day because the roots are just like you. They need to breath some good Florida air too.

7. It isn't necessary to feed when planting, but after about a month to get used to its new surroundings your orange tree will appreciate a good citrus fertilizer. The best rule of thumb here is to wait until there is some new growth.

Once the trees are in the ground you can relax and watch them grow. Citrus will reward you well if you follow a regular feeding schedule, but remember that they are adaptable and not too demanding. It is more important to avoid overfeeding because this can encourage weak growth that looks like a gourmet salad bar to bugs all over the neighborhood, not to mention the diseases looking for a place to call home.

YOUNG TREES, during the first year in a new site, do best with light feeding of a good quality citrus fertilizer every six weeks. Don't feed after September first though because this will result in tender growth that doesn't handle cold winter weather well. Because fertilizer formulas may vary follow the directions on the container. Continue this six week schedule for the second and third year but increase the amount applied.

MATURE TREES should be fed with the same citrus fertilizer three times a year:
January - February
May - June
September - early October, at the latest

There is an easy way to tell if your feeding program is doing well. If the mature leaves are a glossy deep green color and aren't deformed, relax and enjoy the orange juice. If you notice pale or dull coloration or yellow patterning on the leaves you may want to try a little tonic in the form of a nutritional spray with minor elements. This is found in most garden centers and will usually correct the problem.

KEEPING CITRUS HAPPY

We are often asked if mulch can be used around orange trees. The answer is a hesitant yes, but with some precautions. Keep the mulch material at least six inches away from the trunk to help prevent foot rot, a fungus disease that occurs at the soil line. It is also advisable to keep grass from growing up to the trunk for the same reason and a mulch can help to control the grass if you are a winter resident.

Bugs can be a nuisance but rarely a crisis. There are a multitude of natural controls out there helping you. Up north it was almost necessary to spray the fruit trees to prevent codling moth and some others, but citrus can function quite well without chemical intervention.

As an example scale can be a serious problem, but it's the favorite snack of a group of parasitic wasps that lay their eggs on the scaly little devils. As the larva hatch they dine on the scale and kill it. If you look closely at a colony of scale you will probably find a good many dry shells with a little hold drilled in them. Now you know why. The problem is that if you go around spraying high powered insecticides on the scale you also kill the wasps and they were pretty cheap labor.

Mites can sometimes become plentiful but they are seldom a serious problem.

White flies can be a problem but there is no truly effective chemical control. Malathion and Diazinon can help, but again parasitic wasps are working hard to defeat the white fly.

While white fly may resemble botanical dandruff the first sign many folks notice of a white fly, scale or mealybug infestation is a sooty coating on the leaves. This is called sooty mold and does little damage. Once the insect is controlled the excreta that the fungus feeds on is eliminated. A good rain will wash most of the mold away.

Greasy spot is just what it sounds like, greasy spots on the leaves. This is a fungus disease that can cause serious defoliation if it gets out of control. Like most fungus problems it is easier to prevent than cure. Good maintenance, like cleaning up fallen leaves, is the most helpful. Proper watering and a controlled diet are also important. If it becomes a serious problem a good copper spray can help.

Foot rot was mentioned above and this can be fatal if left unchecked. It's important to examine the trunk periodically. Look for wet or dark colored patterns at the soil line. If it has a spongy feel you have a problem. Cut away all the dead tissue and remove the soil to a depth below the infected area. An application of copper fungicide will help stop the infection after it has been cleaned. Again, prevention is the best policy and that means keeping mulch, grass, weeds or debris away from the trunk.

These are only a few of the problems that might arise but it isn't necessary to dwell on the problems, concentrate instead on producing a healthy tree that will give you a plentiful crop of oranges, grapefruit, tangerines, lemons and limes. Don't forget the kumquats.

OFFICIAL FLORIDA CITRUS TEST

Enough of this serious stuff. Let's have a little fun. This is a quiz designed to test your knowledge of trivial little bits of information that can make you look like a know-it-all at the next dinner party. Used properly this random and pointless knowledge can guarantee that you will never have to attend another one of those boring parties.

1. Which of the following is not a member of the citrus family?
   (a) Citron   (b) Kumquat   (c) Mandarin orange   (d) Loquat

2. Who brought the first orange trees to the New World?
   (a) Ponce de   (b) Christopher   (c) Thomas   (d) Hernado
       Leon   Columbus   Jefferson   Cortez

3. Florida produces what percentage of the world's grapefruit?
   (a) 80%   (b) 50%   (c) 35%   (d) 10%

4. The first orange was planted in Florida in 1565. Where?
   (a) Miami   (b) Tampa   (c) Orlando   (d) St. Augustine

5. The grapefruit was developed in the 1700s in?
   (a) The West Indies   (b) China   (c) India   (d) Africa

6. Most citrus are self pollinating.   T   F

7. Tangerines are sometimes referred to as mandarins.   T   F

8. The "key lime" is also known as the "Mexican lime."   T   F

9. The key lime was found growing wild in Florida   T   F
   when the Spanish got here.

10. Grapefruit trees weren't grown in Florida until after   T   F
    the turn of the century.

TROPICAL FRUITS YOU CAN GROW IN FLORIDA

One of the great advantages of living in Florida is that a whole new world of fruit growing is open to you. True you will never grow the same kind of apples or cherries here that you did in Michigan, but it would have been impossible to step out your back door up there and cut some fresh sugar cane, bake a fresh loquat pie or pick your own papayas. The following are only a few of the exotic fruits you can enjoy here.

AVOCADOS are quite comfortable in south Florida and some varieties can even be coaxed into growing in the central region.

BANANAS are about as tropical looking as you can get and there are varieties that will happily inhabit almost every part of the state. They may freeze back to the ground in the winter but return with enthusiasm.

CHERRY OF THE RIO GRANDE and **SURINAM CHERRY** aren't cherries. They are only two members of the plant family, Eugenia. They grow as shrubs or small trees in central and south Florida and in the north they are effective container plants. The fruit is delicious and the flower is also worthwhile. They can also be trained to serve as a hedge.

GUAVAS are great, easy to care for and versatile. They can be pruned to shape, even used as a hedge or grown in containers in the northern part of the state where it gets a little too cold for them.

FIGS can be grown all over the state and there are many excellent varieties to choose from.

KIWI FRUIT grow on a hardy vigorous vine that does well on a trellis. One fact worth noting is that kiwifruit produce male and female flowers on different plants. To harvest a crop you will need both.

LITCHI does well in the southern third of the state and with some cold protection it can be grown in central Florida as well.

LOQUAT is sometimes referred to as Japanese plum. It is a valuable addition to the landscape everywhere in Florida. The spicy scented flowers in winter are followed by delicious yellow fruit in the early spring. Marmalade, pies and dried fruit mixes can all be made from this prolific tropical looking tree.

MACADAMIA nuts can be grown in south Florida but the harvest is not reliable. The attractive tree is still worth the effort though.

MANGO trees are small and well behaved with little maintenance needed. Grafted varieties produce the best fruit but it's fun to start one from seed. The foliage will still be beautiful even if the fruit from your seedling isn't the sweetest. South Florida is mango country but they can do well in most of central Florida as well. They can even be grown as a decorative potted plant in the northern part of the state.

NATAL PLUM is a beautiful shrub from South Africa with a winning combination of deep green leaves, fragrant white flowers and delicious red fruit. It will thrive in central and south Florida and in the northern part of the state it is quite happy in a container.

PAPAYAS grow like weeds in central and south Florida and because they grow so quickly even parts of northern Florida can produce striking tropical looking papaya plants.

PASSION FRUIT is the fruit of the passion vine. There are dozens of varieties that produce delicious fruit and most of them can be grown over much of the state. They have attractive flowers and a vigorous vining habit that earn them a place in the landscape even without the fruit.

PERSIMMON trees are a tradition in the south and they will thrive everywhere in Florida. There are a number of Japanese and hybrid varieties that produce exceptionally well here.

PINEAPPLES were at one time a major agricultural crop in central and south Florida. Today you can grow fruiting varieties and ornamental types anywhere in central and southern parts of the state. There is something special about harvesting your own ripe pineapple. Give this one a try. It's easy.

SAPOATE is sometimes called custard apple. The flavor is unique and the tree is ugly enough to be distinctive. This is a tropical fruit that is happiest in the south but will tolerate temperatures as low as the mid twenties.

STAR FRUIT or **CARAMBOLA** is a small tree that does well in south Florida and with some cold protection thrives in the central part of the state.

SUGAR CANE is just big overgrown grass, but when those family members from Wisconsin or other places where they still shovel snow escape to your house for a week's vacation take them out to the backyard and cut them a piece of fresh sugar cane.

Don't be afraid to try some of these tropical fruits. You can get more information on them from your local library, garden center or agricultural extension office.

HERBS IN FLORIDA

A whole new world is open to you when you begin experimenting with herbs in Florida. Almost all the herbs you grew wherever "up north" was for you will thrive in Florida's mediocre sandy soil. But wait, there's more. Those tender, cold sensitive herbs like aloe vera, sweet fennel and rosemary that had to be coaxed into surviving on the winter windowsill can be a dynamic part of your Florida landscape design.

There are even tropical herbs and spices that will do quite well in most parts of this state. You can grow vanilla, the only edible member of the orchid family, on a trellis or arbor. It's also one of the few vining orchids. Ginger, coffee, tea and sweet olive are all attractive landscape plants with a bonus. You couldn't step out your back door in Pennsylvania and run into growing chocolate plants, carob, allspice, annatto, arrowroot or anise shrub either. Yet these and hundreds more are possible here.

Up north your herb growing was limited to either a dooryard herb garden or the windowsill. It's not the same here. While it's true that a wealth of herbs can be grown better in containers where you have more control over the soil and water, there's a whole lot more potential. The sprawling, informal appearance of many of these plants (like rosemary, thyme and the mints) compliments the casual lifestyle and landscape design that's a key feature of Florida. In the northern and central parts of the state containers are the best way to grow the most cold sensitive herbs and spice plants. During those few chilly days they can be moved into the garage and survive easily. For most, however, some cover on the frosty nights is sufficient.

Most of the herbs you'll grow here you are already familiar with from your herb gardens in the north. You already know that for many of the herbs too much of a good thing like rich soil, fertilizer and water can be detrimental. Because some of the herbs have natural insect repellent talents we suggest that they not be segregated to one little corner of your landscape. Pennyroyal, garlic and dwarf marigolds (tagetes), to mention only a few, deserve a place in your vegetable and flower gardens.

Herb growing has several advantages in Florida. Many of the herbs you might want to include in your garden don't do well in rich, heavy or overly moist soils. We already discussed the ease with which the sand we call soil here in Florida can be modified, acidified, compost enhanced and whatever else you need to do to keep those picky plants happy. You can even provide for the herbs that enjoy wet feet by using a small water garden. There's a lot of flexibility here.

The fact that the growing season is so much longer, (twelve months in most parts of the state) lets you grow even more varieties, some in the cool months and others in the summer heat. There is also the easy possibility of keeping fresh chives, parsley, mint, thyme and basil (just to mention a few) on the table all year.

The following are only suggestions for your Florida herb garden. There are hundreds of herbs available that we haven't listed, and we hope you don't feel insulted if your favorite isn't mentioned, but space is limited. Herbs in Florida is the subject of the next in our Gardening in Florida series.

HERBS FOR THE BEGINNER	HERBS FOR TEAS IN FLORIDA
Basil	Bergamot
Catnip	Chamomile
Chives	Fennel
Dill	Hibiscus
Garlic	Mints (dozens of varieties)
Hot peppers	Pennyroyal
Oregano	Rose
Parsley	Rosemary
Sage	Sasparilla
Thyme	Strawberry
Winter savory	Thea sinensis (real tea)

HERBS FOR THE FLORIDA WINDOWSILL

Aloe vera
Basil
Chives
Mint and catnip
Parsley
Sage
Oregano
Sorrel
Thyme
Watercress
Rocket

HERBS THAT CAN HELP KEEP INSECTS AT BAY

Pennyroyal
Basil
Chives
Dwarf marigold
Tansy
Garlic
Mints
Chamomile
Sage
Catnip
Ornamental hot peppers

TALL BACKGROUND HERBS		LOW AND CREEPING HERBS	
Bergamot	4-6 feet	Chamomile	3-5 inches
Comfey	3 feet	Catnip	12-24 inches
Sage	2-3 feet	Chives	6-10 inches
Sweetbriar (rose)	2-4 feet	Thyme	3-12 inches
Tansy	2-4 feet	Winter savory	10-15 inches
Marsh mallow	3-8 feet	Mints	6-24 inches
Sweet fennel	3-5 feet	Dwarf marigold	6-10 inches
Ginger	3-8 feet	Pennyroyal	6-10 inches
Dill	2-4 feet	Aloe vera	12-18 inches
Rosemary	2-6 feet	Viola	3-6 inches

TROPICAL HERBS AND SPICES FOR FLORIDA

Allspice
Anise shrub
Arrowroot
Capers
Carob
Eucalyptus
Ginger
Hibiscus
Lemon grass
Licorice
Passion fruit
Sasparilla

HERBS FOR THE WATER GARDEN

Arrowhead
Cattail
Lotus
Papyrus (standard and dwarf)
Sweet flag
Water chestnut
Watercress

HERBS THAT ARE A CHALLENGE BUT WELL WORTH THE EFFORT

Calendula (suffers in our heat and humidity)
Chocolate (very cold sensitive)
Coffee (in central and north Florida does well in a container)
Foxglove (heat and humidity take their toll)
Ginseng (north Florida only)
Lavender (there are some varieties that show promise here)
Tea (yes, you can brew a cup from your own plant)
Vanilla (a vining orchid that doesn't like cool weather)

Be adventurous, experiment with some herbs and spices you never grew before; and don't be afraid to plant them in unconventional places. Try growing some of these plants in and around the vegetable plots and flower beds. We have grown strawberries very well as hanging basket plants. Mints and thyme also work well in a hanging basket or container. Many of the herbs make excellent ground covers, some are effective screens and others are beautiful, fragrant or weird enough to be the center of attention in your landscape.

SECTION SEVEN

UNIQUELY FLORIDIAN

When you moved to Florida you moved into some unique situations, problems and opportunities. It takes some time to adjust to the different seasonal patterns, like growing petunias and tomatoes in the winter. Here we leave caladiums and dahlias in the ground, but we dig and chill the tulip bulbs in the refrigerator. Philodendron climb the trees and orchids live in the oaks. All those plants that struggled on the windowsill up north are vigorous members of your landscape down here. We now live in a state that has swaying palms and dramatic magnolias but no lilacs or blue spruce. It boggles the mind.

We can grow oranges and bananas in the backyard but not cherries. We have to worry about salt tolerance, nematode resistance and, yes, even cold damage. Gardeners in Florida don't have it as easy as you might have thought when you were visiting here on vacation. We have some unique problems, and now, they're yours too.

PREVENTING COLD DAMAGE

In a state that's too warm to be temperate, but not quite tropical we can face freeze problems severe enough to almost destroy entire industries. In the early eighties a series of colder than normal winters dealt the citrus growers a blow so serious many were forced out of business. Homeowners who for years had been lulled into a false sense of security also felt the disastrous effects of temperatures in the twenties. Many parts of their ornamental landscape followed the orange groves into botanical oblivion. We would like to point out that is isn't just the temperature drop that can cause cold damage. The number of hours the temperature remains below freezing, the amount of wind, humidity and soil moisture all affect the degree of damage. A light freeze after an unseasonably warm spell where new growth was initiated can be devastating. For many tropical and subtropical plants (Adenium obesum, as an example) there doesn't even need to be a frost to do damage.

Losses due to cold weather and freezing can be minimized by taking some common sense precautions long before the weather forecast causes a panic.

1. Plant hardy species and the most cold resistant varieties of tender plants. As an example the satsuma is one of the most cold tolerant of the oranges.

2. Don't feed with a high nitrogen fertilizer in late autumn. You want your plants to be hardened off and mature so that they can handle the tough times ahead easier. There are winterizer plant food formulas on the market that will provide what your landscape plants need in a last feeding.

3. Keep your plants healthy the rest of the year and they can handle some adverse weather better. Deep watering, mulching, pruning out damaged or diseased wood, planting where there is sufficient sunlight and avoiding overcrowding when planting are all factors in keeping them happy.

4. Tender plants located in low open areas face increased risk of damage from cold weather. The low spots become pockets where temperatures drop the lowest. Windbreaks, fences and hedges can also provide some protection from wind and cold.

5. Protect the roots. Mulch heavily. For some young trees, like citrus, frost cones or mounds of soil around the trunk will help protect from a freeze. Also remember that potted plants have a more exposed root system and are in greater danger from a freeze.

WHAT TO DO WHEN THE COLD WEATHER COMES

If you have done all of the above you have an insurance policy against cold damage, but that doesn't mean that all you have to do when the freezing weather comes is sit by the fireplace and contemplate a cruise to somewhere in the Caribbean where the weather is warmer. We usually have a day or two advance warning that cold temperatures are on the way. This is the time to take some emergency action.

1.   If you have tender container plants they can be moved under cover or into the garage.

2.   Screens or covers of cloth or plastic can be spread over frames you cleverly built around the more sensitive landscape plants earlier when you had some spare time. It is best to keep the fabric or plastic from touching the foliage. If it does contact the foliage there can be some freeze back on that part of the plant. Remember that plastic should be removed during the day or the winter afternoon sun can literally cook the plants you were trying to protect.

3.   Water deeply and early in the day before the cold weather hits. Wet soil holds its heat longer than dry soil does and the plant's tissues are less stressed if the plant has sufficient moisture.

4.   You can provide a little extra heat with a light bulb under your plastic tent, but be very careful with extension cords. Make certain you are following common sense fire safety rules. In larger open areas smudge pots can also be effective. This is the traditional first line of defense employed by theme parks and commercial growers.

5.   Some experts recommend keeping a sprinkler on over night when freezing temperatures are on the way, but this can create other problems, plus add to your water bill. Some claim that leaves encased in ice don't dehydrate in below freezing temperatures like exposed foliage does. Others argue that the ice provides a thermal blanket that keeps the temperature of the leaves from dropping lower.

WHAT YOU CAN DO AFTER THE FREEZE

As soon as the frost has burned off and the sun is shining again we all rush out, pruning shears in hand, to survey the damage. Usually we transplants to this subtropical climate overreact. First we can be thankful you aren't still up north where you would be shoveling snow before you could get to work. Next, relax, have another cup of coffee and take it all in stride. There isn't a lot that you need to do immediately.

1.   Remove the protective covers and plastic sheets before you inadvertently cook the plants you were trying to protect.

2.   Water well. One of the biggest problems with freezing is dehydration.

3.   Don't rush out with fertilizer. Resist the urge to feed until you see some new growth in the spring.

4.   Put the pruning shears away. Wait for new growth then prune by removing damaged wood below the point where dead wood meets green wood. You can use pruning paint on any major wounds if you wish.

5.   Remember when you were living in Maine and the plants would freeze back in the fall and you just sighed and waited until spring? Why is it when we get to Florida we expect every plant to be evergreen and everblooming? Some of the tender perennials like pentas, stokes aster and hosta may freeze back to the soil line, but relax, they'll come back.

Even the hibiscus and other shrubs were merely frost pruned. Don't worry. They'll be fine. Enjoy the invigorating chill in the air and watch a weather report about what it's doing "up there."

PREPARING FOR SUMMER SURVIVAL

If you are among the "snowbirds" that have flocked south for the winter you will enjoy the early spring here then pack up for the great northern migration where you get a second spring. You probably don't even feel guilty about abandoning your landscape during the most trying of times, summer. The heat, humidity, increased insect populations, drought and disease will plague your poor defenseless plants while you're enjoying summer "up there."

There! Have we made you feel guilty enough to give up those plans for a return north? If not there are a few things you can do to help the landscape survive the rigors of summer in Florida. Even if you are a permanent, full time resident these suggestions will make your life easier.

1.   Give one last feeding before you leave. Use a complete fertilizer with slow release nutrients for best results.

2.   Prune to shape and control growth. They will still need a good haircut when you get back, but at least they will look good for awhile.

3.   Check for signs of insects or disease serious enough to pose a threat. We tend to become paranoid about bugs, but they were here long before we arrived and they outnumber us millions to one. They are a part of nature and we need to learn to tell the difference between a few bugs and a serious imbalance in the population. If there is a serious problem spray, dust or apply a slow release systemic insecticide before you leave. You might as well relax and face the facts; plants growing in Florida (and most of the rest of the world too) are going to have bugs, but few six-legged invasions are fatal. In the overall scheme of things Mamma Nature leaves your greenery healthy enough to feed another generation.

4.   Maintenance is your best line of defense. Insects lay their eggs on twigs, seed pods and leaves that then fall to the ground. If you do some basic house cleaning these problems are often minimized.

5.   Water well, wait an hour or so then pull any unsightly weeds. The roots of the offending weeds come free easier in moist soil. Then mulch to help control future weeds. A breathable fabric weed

block is also quite helpful. Moisture, air and nutrients can get through to the roots but most weeds are held in check in their climb toward the sun.

6.	There are drip irrigation systems that are triggered by sensors or rain water gauges that shut the system off when there has been sufficient rain. This can avoid serious drought damage while you are gone and also help to conserve one of our most valuable natural resources, water.

7.	It's a good idea to make arrangements with a friend, neighbor or relative to take care of your lawn and check on the landscape periodically while you are gone. If your friends and neighbors are on vacation or up north for the summer you can also hire a professional maintenance service and they are usually dependable.

8.	If you couldn't resist the urge to purchase tender or demanding plants during the winter visits to the local garden center you can keep them in containers and farm them out to the above mentioned neighbors. Make it sound like you're doing them a favor by allowing your plants to brighten their home grounds.

9.	Potted plants that have given you a winter's worth of beauty can be donated to a local nursing home or charitable institution where they will be appreciated and enjoyed by others. It gives you something to feel good about too.

DEALING WITH DROUGHT

Rather than constantly competing with nature you can try cooperating. It takes a lot of the strain out of Florida gardening and your chances of success are far greater. We know it sounds ridiculous to say a state almost surrounded by water is facing serious water shortages, but the fact is all of us who moved down here, that's you and me, are pulling more water from the aquifer than the rains are replacing. This results in sink holes and salt water intrusion. It is also a fact of life in this subtropical climate that we do have prolonged periods of drought. It really doesn't rain every afternoon, it just seems like it.

When you are planning your landscape keep in mind lawn grasses are the most water demanding component. Y‌‌ ‍ can save water, avoid drought problems and expend a whole lot less effort if you use other groundcovers and massed plantings instead of turf.

Plan your irrigation system to be efficient and simple. A drip system puts the water exactly where it's needed, is inexpensive and easy to install yourself. There are rainwater sensors available that will keep the irrigation from operating if there has been sufficient rain. This can help your water bill too.

When you landscape with drought tolerant plants you can cut the water bills and do your part to conserve our diminishing water supply. You may think this means you've got to use only native plants and weeds but relax. There is a multitude of great xerophytic (drought tolerant) material available, including the following.

Agave	Almost all cacti	Aloe
Asparagus fern	Beauty berry	Bottle brush
Brazilian pepper	Buddleia	Confederate jasmine
Crape myrtle	Croton	Crown-of-thorns
English ivy	Indian hawthorn	Japanese honeysuckle
Jerusalem thorn	Kalanchoe	Lantana
Ligustrum (privet)	Liriope (lily turf)	Loquat
Many pines	Most junipers	Most oaks
Natal plum	Oleander	Oregon grape holly
Pandanus (screw pine)	Pindo palm	Pineapple
Plumeria	Podocarpus	Rhoeo discolor
Rose of sharon	Sable palm	Sansevieria
Sea grape	Silk floss tree	Silverthorn
Southern red cedar	Sweet acacia	Thryallis
Trumpet vine	Wax myrtle	Yucca

Here are some other things you can do to help conserve moisture and deal with drought.

1. Use mulches and ground covers as much as possible and practical. Not only does a colorful ground cover add to the landscape, it can help retain valuable soil moisture.

2. Work large amounts of compost or other organic matter into the soil. Sand isn't efficient at holding water, but compost is.

3. Shade trees also help to retain soil moisture.

4.   Run your sprinklers or other irrigation early in the day before the heat has stressed your plants. Less water is going to be lost to evaporation, more is going to get to the roots.

5.   There are water retaining chemicals you can mix with the soil (you can usually find these at your local flea market) that will help hold moisture if you are going on vacation, but they can deteriorate after a month or two. Be careful not to use too much or you can create a fungus problem from too much moisture.

DROUGHT AND THE LAWN

Turf grasses make the greatest demand in your water bill, but there are several things you can do to limit this demand.

1.   Use alternative ground covers.

2.   Use a sharp blade on your mower. This helps to limit the amount of water lost through a ragged tear and also helps to control the spread of fungus diseases.

3.   Increase the cutting height. This makes a healthier grass plant, provides a denser ground cover to preserve soil moisture and encourages a stronger root system.

4.   During periods of drought avoid using high nitrogen fertilizers. A formula with more potassium will also strengthen the plant's ability to withstand drought stress.

5.   Water only when the turf shows signs of drought stress. Then when you water, apply approximately one inch of water rather than just running the sprinklers for a set period of time. This is called "drought conditioning" and after following a watering program like this for a month or so you will find that water demand will be considerably less.

SALT IN THE SOIL, AIR AND WATER

One of the problems we encounter living on a little finger of land almost surrounded by sea water is salt. Salt that's trapped in the coastal soils, blows in on the brisk sea winds and flows into our coastal aquifers. Many of the plants we would like to include in our landscapes gradually decline and eventually die from salt poisoning.

As the underground fresh water supply continues to diminish more and more salt water seeps into the aquifers. This means folks that had no salt problems because they were near but not directly on the sea coast now have salt in their well water. This is a problem that will most likely get worse so we might as well learn to live with it and concentrate on planting landscape material that will accept salty soil or water. The following is only a partial list. You can get more detailed information from your local agricultural extension office, garden club, library or garden center.

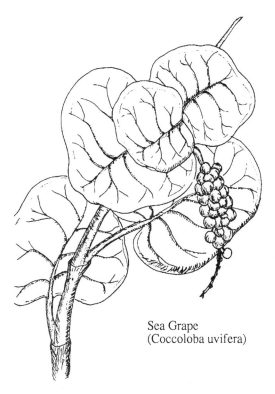

Sea Grape
(Coccoloba uvifera)

trees, shrubs and plants are very salt tolerant and can be grown almost on the beachfront.

Agave	Aloe	Cabbage palm
Coconut	Crown-of-thorns	Hottentot fig
Natal plum	Oleander	Pinguin (pineapple kin)
Pittosporum	Portia tree	Sansevieria
Sea grape	Sea hibiscus	Silverthorn
Some cacti	Wedelia	Yucca

Back from the dunes where salt concentrations are much lower there is a wealth of plant material that thrives or at least tolerates these conditions. These are sometimes referred to as "somewhat tolerant" and can show a good deal of stress when planted where there is too much salt or the water contains seriously high salts. Among the moderately salt tolerant plants you might want to consider are the following.

Black olive	Bottle brush	Brazilian pepper
Croton	Date palm	Holly fern
Indian hawthorn	Ixora	Kalanchoe
Lantana	Leather leaf fern	Liriope
Live oak	Loquat	Magnolia
Many cacti	Oregon grape holly	Pandanus (screw pine)
Pindo palm	Plumeria	Podocarpus
Rhoeo discolor	Some of the junipers	Southern red cedar
Washington palm	Wax myrtle	Yaupon holly

If there are plants you wish to grow, and you live in an area where there are salt concentrations in the soil, you can use containers and purchase prepared soils or salt free compost. Problems may still arise if you can't provide salt free water or there is a salt spray carried by the wind.

WHAT'S ALL THAT FUNNY STUFF
GROWING IN THE TREES?

It's hard to believe that Spanish moss is a cousin to the pineapple, but it's a fact. They are both bromeliads. The pineapple is the only edible member of the family, but there are a lot of interesting kin. Spanish moss is an epiphyte, this means it gathers its moisture and nutrient requirements from the atmosphere. Spanish moss isn't parasitic. It is doing no harm whatsoever to your little oak tree. Spanish moss is a part of the charm of the south. Many of us Yankees come down here and set about making our Florida homestead look like the backyard we left behind. And we start with these poor innocent gray beards that lend an air of dignity to the sprawling live oaks. Don't give in to this primitive urge to yank it out of your trees. Relax and enjoy it.

We have seen folks so set on destroying this poor plant that they employed high powered sprayers to pump copper sulfate to the top of their trees. Sure enough the poison killed most of it, but the dead moss was still hanging there and it looked terrible. Not to mention the futility of the exercise because in less than a month seedlings were sprouting and Mama Nature was busy planting her garden again.

Take some time to examine these remarkable plants that don't grow in the north (at least no farther north than Virginia). Their leaves are coated with a spongy material that absorbs dew, rain drops or nutrient laden water dripping from the tree leaves above. They produce tiny flowers and fuzzy seeds that float through the air on gentle Florida breezes until they come in contact with a place they would like to settle down. That may be your crape myrtle, a power line or some ancient oak. They produce no roots that invade the tree they live on and do absolutely no harm.

You might also find another member of the same family growing on your trees, ball moss forms a sphere around the twig or wire and again sets up housekeeping without doing any damage. Ball moss is another part of the natural landscape in Florida. Don't destroy it.

FLORIDA HAS A LOT OF BUGS

You may have noticed, and we probably don't need to remind you, but there's an unwritten rule that you can't write a gardening book without discussing bugs. To fulfill this obligation here is the last word on Florida bugs. True we have mosquitoes, but we've seen bigger ones in Pennsylvania. Also true, fleas, ticks and chiggers never sleep in our almost permanent spring, but these pests are found everywhere. All states have plenty of wasps, hornets and yellow jackets. What we do have over most of the rest of the country is fire ants, and they can be a serious problem because they are smarter than us. When we poison their nest they just move. We develop special poisons for the queen, and they produce nests with multiple queens. If you eliminate one colony they set up three or four more to replace it.

Florida folks complain about all these but they aren't what bothers them the most. Nope, the LOVEBUG is the subject of more complaint and conversation than any other insect in this state. Lovebugs (for the technically addicted, Plecia neartica) are little black flies that mass along highways and splatter themselves against your windshield as a part of their mating ritual. As is the case with many of the critters Floridians don't like, the natives claim they came from somewhere else. In this case these pesky little March flies (another name for lovebugs) came from Louisiana and were first reported in Florida in 1947.

They get romantic twice a year, first in April or May, then again during August or September. The poor adults only live two or three days but during that time the female lays several hundred eggs in decaying vegetation.

The larvae are beneficial because they help in the decomposition process by feeding on dead plant matter. They are busy turning it into useful nutrients. The adults don't have time to eat dinner so they pose no threat to your landscape. All isn't fun and games for these little beasts though. The young are a favorite meal for robins, quail and many other birds. Life ain't easy when you're a little bug.

Florida is also home to a thriving bee industry and honey made from orange blossoms is delightful. One more observation on this state's notorious insect population; we have an unbelievable number of moths and butterflies fluttering among our flower beds, shrubbery and herb gardens. Not all bugs are bad, most are beneficial and many are beautiful. Don't be afraid to get to know a few of them. They can make good neighbors.

THE GOOD, THE BAD AND THE UGLY

We automatically think all insects are bad guys but most are no threat to our way of life and some are even beneficial. Among the good bugs are:

Ant lions—as larvae they dig little traps in the sand and catch ants.

Most spiders—aren't insects but they are in the same classification we generally refer to technically as "creepy crawlies." They trap and devour in most diabolical ways flies, moths and other insects that do have a bad reputation.

Honey bees—make honey and work diligently pollinating our crop plants while trying to provide for their kids. In return we rob their homes of the honey they put aside for rainy days and their kids' future.

Predatory wasps and hornets—consume great numbers of harmful bugs even though they pose a threat when we violate their space.

Parasitic wasps—lay their eggs on aphids, caterpillars and other crawling packages of baby food. The egg hatches and the young eat their way to adulthood and in the process destroy the reluctant host.

Assassin bugs, wheel bugs, ground beetles and earwigs—all regularly dine on other bugs.

Earthworms—do a lot more than serve as bait for some poor unsuspecting bass. They break down organic matter, aerate the soil and feed the robins.

Praying mantis—are famous for their predatory religious practices.

Syrphid flies—as adults may resemble small hornets but the young are an ugly green larvae that devours aphids at the rate of about one per minute.

Butterflies and moths—by the thousands pollinate wild flowers and crops alike, provide food for songbirds and delight young and old with their grace and beauty.

Thousands of other insects convert fallen leaves into soil, chew dead limbs and tree trunks into sawdust, feed on invasive plants we call weeds, devour insect enemies, feed birds, small mammals, reptiles, frogs, toads and even some fish.

The Good

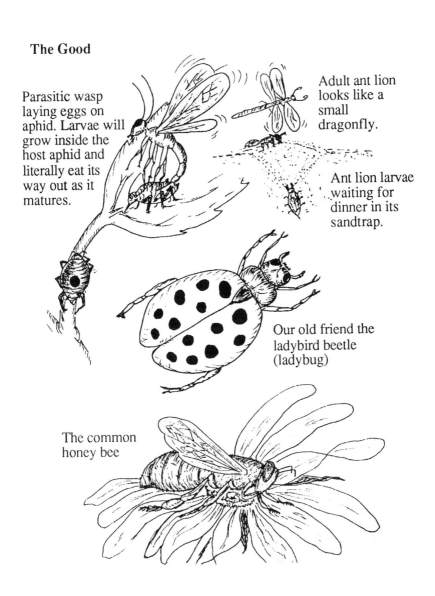

Parasitic wasp laying eggs on aphid. Larvae will grow inside the host aphid and literally eat its way out as it matures.

Adult ant lion looks like a small dragonfly.

Ant lion larvae waiting for dinner in its sandtrap.

Our old friend the ladybird beetle (ladybug)

The common honey bee

The Bad

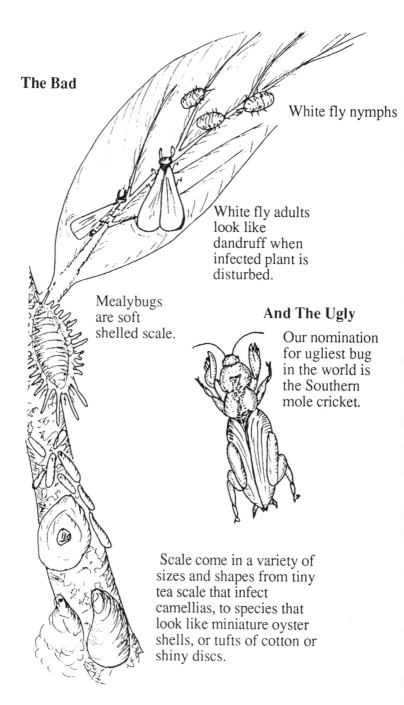

White fly nymphs

White fly adults
look like
dandruff when
infected plant is
disturbed.

Mealybugs
are soft
shelled scale.

And The Ugly

Our nomination
for ugliest bug
in the world is
the Southern
mole cricket.

Scale come in a variety of
sizes and shapes from tiny
tea scale that infect
camellias, to species that
look like miniature oyster
shells, or tufts of cotton or
shiny discs.

Up north we knew all about weeds like dandelions and ragweed, crabgrass and chickweed. Well, guess what? Florida's got all of those beauties and more. Among the multitude of weeds this state offers are these gems.

SANDSPUR (Cenchrus spp.) is a weed grass that cleverly flattens itself out along the ground so a mower will miss it. The spiny seeds can discourage going barefoot in the park.

KUDZU (pueraria lobata) is north Florida's public enemy number one. This weed vine is an Asian import that grows faster than Jack's beanstalk and has no natural enemies. It can completely overrun a pine forest in a few short years.

MELALEUCA (several varieties) is sometimes called punk tree. It has a spongy papery bark and an ability to spread that rivals the kudzu. This is one of south Florida's biggest problems because it completely overwhelms the native plants and also because it is a serious fire hazard.

Sandspur

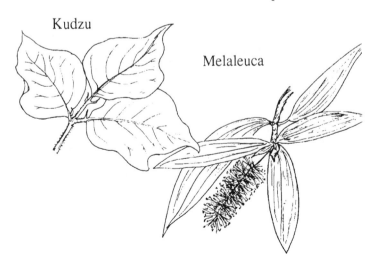

Kudzu

Melaleuca

ANSWERS TO QUIZZES

HOW WELL DO YOU KNOW YOUR BULBS, TUBERS AND CORMS? (page 33)

1. False, the foliage is needed after the current bloom is done to manufacture the energy and food required to produce the next season's flowers.
2. False, while many of the plants we call bulbs are more properly tubers (example: caladiums), rhizomes (iris) or corms (glads) there are many true bulbs besides the lily. Onions, garlic, amaryllis, narcissi and tulips to name a few.
3. True
4. True
5. True
6. False, they will bloom all summer long.
7. False
8. False, but you can plant at two week intervals to have an extended blooming season.
9. False, dahlias will grow quite well in most areas of Florida.
10. True

FLORIDA PALMS (page 48)

1. False, palm honey is popular because of its uniquely delightful and mellow flavor.
2. True
3. True
4. False, the milk in a coconut is nature's way of guaranteeing the sprouting seed (yes, the coconut is a seed) sufficient moisture to send a root in search of water.
5. True, the needle palm is a rugged and attractive native palm.
6. False, while most palms are salt tolerant, they don't require salt to grow.
7. True
8. False, palms that produce a solitary trunk usually die if the heart is damaged.
9. True
10. False, bamboo is a member of the grass family.

OFFICIAL FLORIDA CITRUS TEST (page 141)

1. (d)
2. (b)
3. (a)
4. (d)
5. (a)
6. True, although many of the crosses, like the tangelo, will produce more with a pollinator.
7. True
8. True
9. False, it escaped and ran wild throughout the West Indies.
10. False, the first grapefruit tree in Florida was planted near Tampa in 1823.

We hope you will enjoy gardening in Florida and hope that this book has helped to answer a few of your questions. We also encourage you to call on the experts, visit your local library, agricultural extension office and botanical gardens. Chat with your neighbors and local garden center staff. By the way, it's okay to be homesick for the lilacs in the spring.

HELP!

This book isn't intended to provide you with all the answers. In fact, our objective is only to stimulate some interest in gardening in Florida and help newcomers to the state feel comfortable with what grows here. The more active your involvement with subtropical horticulture the more questions are going to come to mind. No need to worry though because, as we have been telling you in almost every chapter, there's lots of help at hand.

The University of Florida has a Cooperative Extension Service office in every county in the state. If some bug you don't know invited himself to dinner the local extension office can tell you all about him. There is a wealth of information to be found here and you can be a part of it. They have a MASTER GARDENER PROGRAM and when you complete the course you are a certified Master Gardener. You can then help others become successful with their landscaping and aid them in solving their problems. Contact your local office for details.

Many of these local extension offices also produce periodic newsletters that provide useful information on seasonal activities, local events and recent research on horticultural subjects.

You say the roses don't look as happy now as they did when you planted them? The folks at the extension office can help, but there is probably a local chapter of the Florida Rose Society to call on as well. Perhaps you are in a quandary as to what tree is going to do well in your backyard. Contact your local garden club. Who knows? You might even decide to join. Garden clubs are a great way to meet nice people (most plant people are extremely nice) and cultivate friendships. Not only do you make friends, you can even get those questions answered. If your local garden club isn't listed in the phone book check the calendar of events in the newspaper for their next meeting or contact the chamber of commerce. You can also contact the FLORIDA FEDERATION OF GARDEN CLUBS, 1400 S. Denning Drive, Winter Park, FL 32789. They are eager to put you in touch with your local club.

Your local library should have a wealth of gardening information as well as listings of all the plant societies, both statewide and national. There is a very active Florida Camellia Society, Florida Herb Society, Florida Native Plant Society and Florida Rose Society, to name only a few. Many of these societies not only provide information but also swap plants and seeds.

Very likely there is a garden correspondent or columnist writing for your local newspaper and they also provide up to the minute information of Florida gardening. Many of them also answer readers' questions in their columns. These local writers can be a valuable resource for you.

There are also some good books to be found in your local library, bookstore and better garden centers. The following are just a few. Again we apologize if we have omitted a favorite.

FLORIDA LANDSCAPE PLANTS, by Watkins and Sheehan is the premier book on Florida gardening. This should be on every gardener's book shelf.

YOUR FLORIDA GARDEN, by Watkins and Wolf, is an excellent companion text to "Florida Landscape Plants." It's filled with useful information.

FLORIDA HOME GROWN: LANDSCAPING, by Tom MacCubbin contains valuable charts and solid home grown information. He also wrote a companion text, THE EDIBLE LANDSCAPE, which covers a wealth of tropical and subtropical plants grown for food.

GROWING AND USING EXOTIC FOODS, by Marian Van Atta is more than a good source of information, it's a good read too. Marian also wrote another great book, GROWING FAMILY FRUIT AND NUT TREES.

CITRUS GROWING IN FLORIDA by Larry Jackson is one of the best texts available on citrus cultivation.

XERISCAPING, by Monica Brandies is one of the most recent and readable guides to the use of drought tolerant and native plants. This one is valuable reading.

FLORIDA CRITTERS, by Bill Zak is a great guide to Florida's insect pests. He helps you identify them and tells you how to control them too.

FLORIDA GARDENING: THE NEWCOMER'S SURVIVAL MANUAL, another good book by Monica Brandies, makes a good companion to this text. She covers such topics as landscape design and houseplants in Florida.